WINE BUYERS GUIDE

WINE BUYERS GUIDE

CLIFTON FADIMAN
SAM AARON
EDITED BY DARLENE GEIS

HARRY N. ABRAMS, INC.
PUBLISHERS · NEW YORK

ULRICH RUCHTI, DESIGNER
RUTH EISENSTEIN, ASSOCIATE EDITOR

Library of Congress Cataloging in Publication Data

Fadiman, Clifton
   Wine buyers guide

   Includes index.
   1. Wine and wine making. I. Aaron, Sam, joint
author. II. Fadiman, Clifton
         III. Title.
TP548.F24   641.2′2   76-47678
ISBN 0-8109-1754-8
ISBN 0-8109-2063-8 pbk.

Library of Congress Catalogue Card Number: 76-47678

Published in 1977 by Harry N. Abrams, Incorporated, New York

Printed and bound in Japan

(Frontispiece) A Young Bacchant, bronze by Jean-Baptiste Carpeaux
The Christian Brothers Collection

CONTENTS

A NOTE ABOUT THIS BOOK

This concise, up-to-date *Wine Buyers Guide* by the authors of *The Joys of Wine* offers all the wine lore necessary to enable the vastly increasing society of American wine lovers to buy, store, serve, drink, enjoy, and judge their wine with prudence and pleasure.

Full-color maps, reproductions of labels, and "How to Read a Wine Label" features are provided for California, New York, France, and Germany. Added to the information about every significant American vineyard and the wine districts of France, Germany, Italy, Spain, and Portugal are our recommendations for specific wines and their approximate prices. As for the wine countries of the rest of the globe, we have given names and prices of good wines that are fairly widely distributed in the United States. The updated vintage chart covers the most important wine-producing countries of the world and the vintages of the past twenty years.

Leading off this volume, somewhat condensed, is the essay on wine "Brief History of a Love Affair," which appeared originally in *Holiday* magazine in 1957. It attempts to sum up for wine lovers of all seasons the pleasures to be found in a lifelong involvement with the grape.

CLIFTON FADIMAN

SAM AARON

BRIEF HISTORY OF A LOVE AFFAIR

Dead Lucre: burnt Ambition: Wine is best.

—HILAIRE BELLOC, Heroic Poem in Praise of Wine

Like most love stories, mine will mean something to lovers; rather less to those merely capable of love; to the incapable, nothing. And, since no love affair's wild heart lets itself be netted in words, this chronicle of a passion may likewise fail of effect. Yet what lover, telling his tale, has ever been put off by the thought of failure? For he speaks not to persuade but to dress his delight in another guise, and, if he cannot command attention, will settle for being overheard. If his defective audience-sense often makes him a bore, it is a risk he runs cheerfully enough.

In successful love affairs the most radiant moment often occurs at the outset. Consummation, repetition, recollection: each diffuses its appropriate delight. Incomparable, however, is the moment when, all innocent of experience, knowledge, and judgment, one for the first time meets the object of a future passion and feels chosen, marked, almost *fated*.

Paris in 1927: of all places on the round earth's varied crust the best place in which to try one's first bottle. My wife had by a few weeks preceded me there, so that when I arrived she was already wearing the city like a glove. We met at noon of a brilliant August day, a day like a pearl. We had little money but much youth. For our lunch my wife, shrewdly deciding to

A country wine can be enjoyed without formality

Facing: But a legendary Château Lafite must be experienced with reverence

start me off modestly, chose the Bon Marché, the Macy's of the Left Bank. She could have saved her pains: I was in Paris: a department store was Aladdin's palace. Was the lunchroom on the fourth floor? Or in Heaven? I have forgotten.

With our lunch my wife, already to me formidably learned in these matters, ordered a cheap white Graves. Its deep straw color was pleasing to the eye. Even in this busy department store it was served with just a graceful allusion to a flourish. It was properly chilled against the midsummer heat. For the first time I tasted *wine*. It must have sent me into a mild catatonia for it was not until perhaps sixty seconds later that I seemed to hear my wife's voice say from far away, "You have the most peculiar, *foolish* smile on your face." "Do I?" was all I could reply. We may know we are happy when we do not know we are smiling.

And so the die was cast. I felt not so much that here was a new experience as that here was an old experience that had been waiting all my life for me to catch up with it. It was almost enough to make one credit Plato's crazy doctrine of reminiscence.

When one is young and has little money it is prudent to spend that little on the unnecessary, the emotional dividends being higher. We stayed six weeks in Paris and a large part of our budget went on wine that, I am proud to say, we could not afford.

By the time I had finished my tenth bottle in Paris and could tell claret from Burgundy without glancing at the bottle's shoulder slope, I had grasped a fundamental fact: that the pleasures of wine, being both sensory and intellectual, are profound. There are few pleasures of which this can be said.

The appeal to the senses may be simple; one can toss off a glass of a *vin de carafe* with mild pleasure, and so an end. But it *need* not be: there is wine available (nor should one drink too much of it) proffering a whole world of complex stimuli involving taste, color, and fragrance. Add to this the fact that one tastes a wine in several different ways, all involved in a single swallow, for this swallow leads a triple life: one in the mouth, another in the course of slipping down the gullet, still another, a beautiful ghost, the moment afterward.

This much I learned quickly. Nor have I ever tired of learning it again and again. The sensory satisfactions of wine, varying with each sip, each bottle, each occasion, are so ramified that boredom is impossible.

The intellectual attractions of wine are less quickly understood. At twenty-three I did not grasp them at all, and I am still but a grade school student. The fact is that, like philosophy or law or mathematics, wine is a *subject*, or what Arnold Toynbee would call an intelligible field of study. The easiest way to comprehend this idea is to realize that one can *talk* about wine, and on a dozen planes, from the simple one of an exchange of likes and dislikes, to more complex ones involving the careful analysis of sensations, together with such fields of inquiry as history, geography, topography, physics, chemistry, law, and commerce. Name me any liquid—except our own blood—that flows more intimately and incessantly through the labyrinth of symbols we have conceived to mark our status as human beings, from the rudest peasant festival to the mystery of the Eucharist. To take wine into our mouths is to savor a droplet of the river of human history.

The Founding Fathers, if recollection serves, were all wine drinkers; some subtle coarsening, a slight lowering of the national tone, made its entrance with Andrew Jackson and his gang of corn-liquor devotees. H. Warner Allen's claim may seem a trifle expansive, but surely not absurd: "Main Street would vanish if all its inhabitants drank half a bottle of wine with each meal."

As a subject one can as easily finish with wine as with Shakespeare. There is always more to be learned and therefore more to be communicated, for wine does not isolate but binds men together. As one drinks more and better bottles many mental processes are called into play—memory, imagination, judgment, comparison are but a few. Even volition is involved, as when one summons the will power not to acquiesce in the opinions of other wine drinkers, or refuses to be bluffed by the prestige of a year or label. At such moments one may even claim to be performing a moral act.

I believe these things deeply, just as, like any sensible person, I discount the abracadabra of wine: the excesses of connoisseurship, the absurdities of finicky service, the ceremonial of a hierachy of glasses, the supposed ability of the expert to determine from a few sips which side of the hill the original grapes were grown on. One can make excellent love in a meager hall bedroom, the requisite elements being three: two lovers and a means of support. So with wine, the requisite elements being likewise three: a bottle, which may be a country-wench Rhône, surrendering at once its all, or a magisterial Romanée Conti, calling for involved investigation; a glass, preferably thin, clean, and holding at least half a pint; and a lover. (Perhaps I should add a corkscrew.)

But, because wine may be enjoyed without hoopla, that does not mean that care should not be taken in its consideration. Wine is elemental, not elementary.

This said, the time would seem to have come for a short, testy digression on those two opposed figures, the wine snob and the wine *sans-culotte*.

It is easy to make fun of the wine snob. It is also often good fun. Everyone recalls James Thurber's caption to his drawing showing one would-be connoisseur offering his dinner guests a glass of wine: "It's a naive domestic Burgundy without any breeding, but I think you'll be amused by its presumption." Such silliness exists, and should be laughed out of court. On the other hand a "wine snob" may simply be someone who knows more about wine than I do—I meet him frequently—and has not yet learned to convey his information tactfully or clothe his enthusiasm in quiet English. But we must qualify further. Thurber's

"It's a naive domestic Burgundy without any breeding, but I think you'll be amused by its presumption."

13

popinjay *is* a popinjay—and yet the word "breeding," which may seem affectation, has a fairly definite meaning. It is part of the slang of wine lore. A good Châteauneuf-du-Pape may boast a dozen excellent qualities, including its moderate price. Taste it, however, after a first-rate Latour and it is not difficult to sense that the claret is clothed in a certain unaggressive elegance to which the forthright Rhône makes no claim. The plain fact is that wine has personality. It is not dead matter, like a motorcar, but a live thing, like a human being or a page of fine prose.

The wine snob at his worst is a bit of a bore and a bit of a fool. But at least he is a learned bore and a learned fool. The wine *sans-culotte* is a complete bore and a complete fool. He is opposed to a hierarchy of taste (even when it is patiently explained to him that this is not a fixed hierarchy) as his kin spirit is opposed to a hierarchy of political competence. So widespread among us is the notion that the only way to discover the right standard is to count the noses of those adhering to it, that even wine dealers, who know better, and writers on wine, who know much better, give lip service to such dogmas as "A wine is good if it tastes good" or "A good wine is the wine you like." Back of these statements probably lies the idea that they will make converts to wine by making wine seem as accessible, as "democratic," as orange pop.

Yet the very wine man who, for what he thinks sound commercial reasons, expounds this nonsense will spend a great deal of his time contradicting it by his actions. For he is constantly offering his friends, not the wine they will "like" or that he thinks they will "like," but simply the best wine he has, in the conviction that the palate is as educable as the mind or the body.

Few men can afford to drink only the best; and indeed no man should want to, for there is a certain monotony in excellence, as there is in mediocrity. But that need not hinder a man, even as he sips his sound, cheap wine, from knowing that there are other wines capable of giving him, if he has paid any attention to his palate, rarer and finer pleasures. A wine is not good merely because I like it. It is perfectly possible however that I may like it because it is not good; in which case it is pointless for me to change the wine before changing myself.

These intemperate remarks off my chest, I return to the narrative of my small *affaire*. I

Scenes from the wine harvest
The Christian Brothers Collection

record here, not information, but merely the birth and growth of an emotion. The small store of knowledge I possess I did not begin to accumulate until about seven years after my return from Paris.

I learned that most of the few simple rules about drinking wine are not chichi but sensible conclusions drawn from hundreds of years of experience of intelligent men. I learned also that these rules are not inflexible. It is standard practice, and good practice, to marry Chablis to shellfish, but the best Chablis I ever tasted was a superchilled bottle drunk in defiant gulps, unaccompanied by any food, on a very hot day when I was very thirsty. One morning at 3 a.m., tired and famished after eight hours at my writing desk, I ravished the kitchen and ate two cans of unheated Vienna sausages on Vermont crackers, together with a whole bottle of Chassagne-Montrachet '45. Barbarous? Not at all—merely an instance controverting Robert Browning, with

. . . the time and the place
And the loved one all together!

I suppose no account of a happy marriage can be, except to the participants, notably interesting. I shall hurry over mine. The changing embodiments of my spouse have on occasion disappointed me: some, the termagants, developed an acid temper; the reputed charms of others faded upon consummation. Many were not worth the bride-purchase price. With still others, though good of their kind, I found myself, after a decent interval of connubial experiment, temperamentally incompatible. I shall never learn to love the lady known as Vouvray, for example, and I gladly surrender all rosé wines to their admirers. Yes, we have had our ups and downs, wine and I, our misunderstandings and our reconciliations, our delights and our discords. On the whole however I think of ourselves as a model couple: faithful, mutually solicitous, still ardent, and, in the case of the lady, well-preserved.

The record of our union is contained in my Cellar Book, the earliest entry being that of October 17, 1935, at which time I seem to have laid down a dozen Morey, Clos de Lambrays '29 at a price ($28) that today induces wistful dreams. "Quite beautiful" is the notation under "Remarks": vague phrasing, but from the heart. The day before yesterday I binned three cases

that for some years had been maturing their charms for my special benefit: Volnay, Clos des Ducs '43; Niersteiner Rehbach '43 (which may be *too* mature—it is such delicate uncertainties that give to wine drinking what hazards give to golf); and Piesporter Goldtröpfchen Schloss Marienlay '47. Between these two entries lies a third of a lifetime of adventures, each one drawn by the twist of a corkscrew from its horizontal torpor in the dim cellar to the vivid life awaiting it within the clear glass.

The drinking of wine seems to me to have a moral edge over many other pleasures and hobbies in that it promotes love of one's neighbor. As a general thing it is not a lone occupation. A bottle of wine begs to be shared; I have never met a miserly wine lover. The social emotions it generates are equidistant from the philatelist's solitary gloating and the football fan's gregarious hysteria. "Wine was not invented," says J. M. Scott. "It was born. Man has done no more than learn to educate it." In other words, wine is alive, and when you offer it to your fellow man you are offering him life. More than that, you are calling out more life in him, you are engaging in what might be called creative flattery, for you are asking him to summon up his powers of discrimination, to exercise his taste, or perhaps merely to evince curiosity or a desire to learn. I know no other liquid that, placed in the mouth, forces one to think.

But, if such considerations seem too rarefied, I retreat to my last line of defense, that of enlightened selfishness. I heard once, or perhaps read somewhere, that the palate is among the last of our organs to decay. I do not know whether this is so; I am not so great a fool as to hand over to the Inquisition of science a statement that has all the marks of a self-evident truth. Yes, our muscles give way at last to gravity's quiet, resistless pull; the best, the most joyful of our glands, in the end withers; the eye, the ear lose some of their fine quick power to seize upon the world; the limbs begin to ask What's the hurry? But I know men of eighty whose infirmities for the brief space of a bottle's emptying vanish as they sip their wine, their taste buds as lively as when they were one-and-twenty—nay, livelier. The pleasures of old age are few, but what one is more worthy of cultivation than a pleasure that the body, even in decay, can enjoy without enfeeblement, and judgment and memory still lift to the plane of the nonmaterial?

I turn the pages of my Cellar Book. Two lines, appearing toward the end of *The Waste Land*, slip unbidden into my mind:

London Bridge is falling down falling down falling down

. . .

These fragments I have shored against my ruins

. . .

C. F.

Brother Timothy, cellar master of The Christian Brothers, brings his expertise to the tasting of a wine

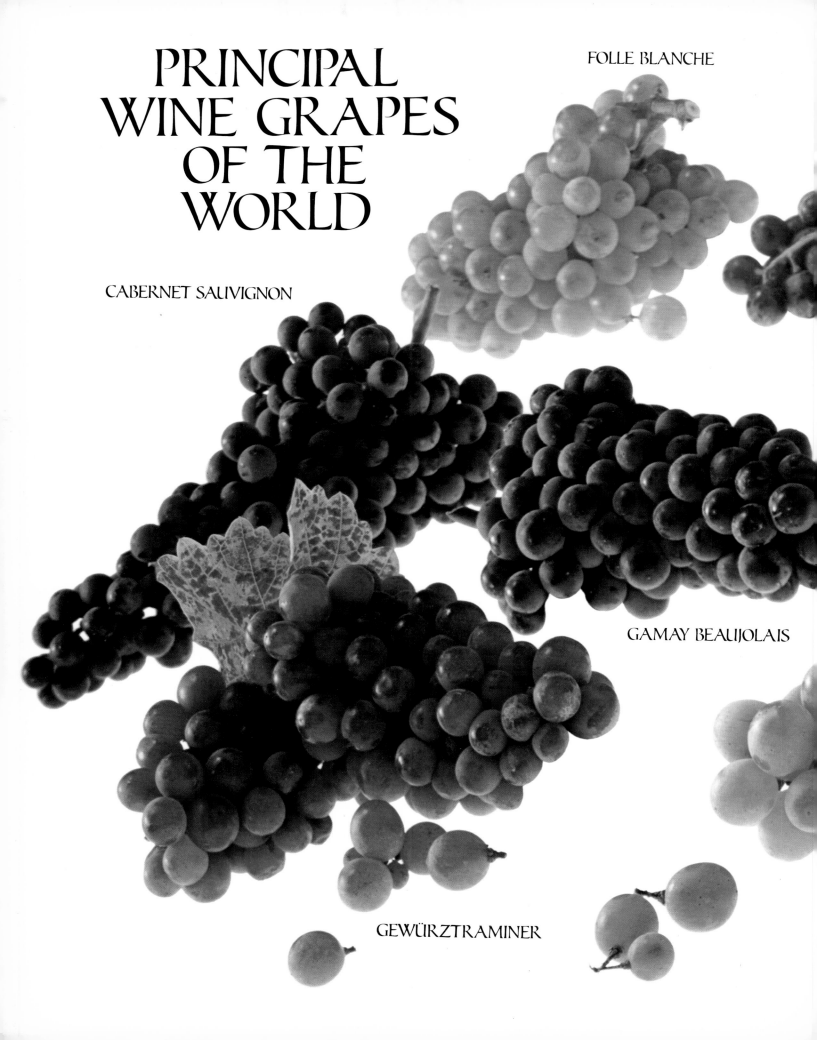

PRINCIPAL WINE GRAPES OF THE WORLD

FOLLE BLANCHE

CABERNET SAUVIGNON

GAMAY BEAUJOLAIS

GEWÜRZTRAMINER

JOHANNISBERG RIESLING

GRENACHE

CHENIN BLANC

PINOT NOIR

SAUVIGNON BLANC

In California	Comments
The pride of the finest North Coast plantings.	The basic grape of Lafite, Mouton, and Haut-Brion, as well as of most of the other great red Bordeaux. Its wine is long-lived, beautifully balanced, with much power and class—certainly the best red wine of California.
Limited production, owing to low yields and rather high costs. Particularly successful in Napa, Sonoma, and Mendocino counties, and south of the Bay Area.	Has not yet achieved the heights of the Cabernet Sauvignon in California, but is on the way. Its wine is similar to the French red Burgundies but lighter and drier.
Ever-increasing plantings from northern Mendocino to southern Monterey County.	Despite its name, which may tend to confuse, Gamay Beaujolais is actually an offshoot of the Pinot Noir grape. Yields a wine that is fruity, fresh, and quick to mature.
Called Napa Gamay in California. Grows in the North Coast counties and the warmer Central Valley.	Although often confused with the Gamay Beaujolais (above), not in the same class. An economical grape because the yield per acre is high. Provides only modest depth and character, but resulting wine, never outstanding, can be light and agreeable.
A good basic grape of Napa and Sonoma counties, now being planted profusely in the warmer Central Valley.	If it comes from Napa or Sonoma County, you will usually find the wine excellent: deep-colored and full-bodied. Satisfactory but not nearly so good when the source is the Central Valley. Often better than its Italian counterpart.
Grows best in the North Coast counties, but is planted all over the state.	America's basic wine grape—fruity, quick to mature. Provides the varietal foundation for the best jug wines.
Responsible for the excellent vins rosés of the North Coast counties. Also used for jug wine in Central Valley and in making the best port of California.	The best California rosé and red jug wines owe their origin to this grape, which yields a fresh, pleasant, well-balanced wine. Used for jug wine in the San Joaquin Valley.
Planted almost exclusively in northern California, where the wine is called Pinot Chardonnay.	High quality, but the yield per acre very low. The wine is not as fruity and a bit drier than the French white Burgundies. Topflight examples can hold their own against Chassagne-Montrachet, Meursault, and Pouilly-Fuissé.
Thrives only in the cooler sections of the northern counties.	Only the true Riesling grape in California bears the prefix "Johannisberg." This distinguishes it from the many imitators that bear the word "Riesling" but not "Johannisberg." Fruit and bouquet are less pronounced than in Germany or Alsace.
At its best in Sonoma, Napa, Santa Clara, San Benito, and Monterey counties.	Generally pale in color and on the dry side (with few exceptions), superb bouquet—hence often used in California champagne blends.
Grows in the North Coast counties and upper Central Valley.	Generally yields a wine similar to French Graves. Often sold as California Dry Sauterne and Blanc-Fumé.
Generally is limited to the North Coast counties.	Whether European or Californian, Traminer wines are generally soft, showing a bit of sweetness, and with pronounced flowery bouquet. For the best of the harvest the growers often substitute the legally permitted alternative name "Gewürztraminer."
Grows in North Coast area and upper Central Valley.	In France, provides a wine high in acid, excellent for making cognac. Happily, in California it yields a pale, very dry light white that can be delightful. Often bears the label "Chablis" or "French Colombard" when source is California. Sometimes it makes a slightly sweet wine.
Grows in the North Coast counties and Central Valley.	Gros Plant du Nantais is well known and similar to Muscadet. The wine Folle Blanche makes in California is tart and refreshing; sometimes bottled as a varietal.

ZINFANDEL

PINOT CHARDONNAY

RED WINES

Variety	Quality	In Europe
CABERNET SAUVIGNON	Excellent	Dominates in all the better Bordeaux vineyards.
PINOT NOIR	Very good	No wine in France is entitled to the name Burgundy unless it is made from 100 percent Pinot Noir—one of the noblest of red-wine grapes.
GAMAY BEAUJOLAIS	Very good	Not to be confused with Gamay (listed below), which is the grape of Beaujolais. The Gamay Beaujolais is unique to California.
GAMAY	Fair	There are many subvarieties. The best grows in Beaujolais. Also the basic grape of many other European vineyards.
BARBERA	Good	Grows in North Italy.
ZINFANDEL	Good	European origin unknown. Now unique to California.
GRENACHE	Good	The grape of Tavel Rosé, most of the Côtes du Rhône, and some of Châteauneuf-du-Pape. Widely planted in the Rioja of Spain.

WHITE WINES

Variety	Quality	In Europe
CHARDONNAY (also, improperly, Pinot Chardonnay)	Excellent	Grows in Burgundy, Chablis, Champagne, and parts of Italy.
JOHANNISBERG RIESLING	Excellent	Grows in the Rhine and Moselle valleys of Germany and in Alsace, Austria, Luxembourg, and North Italy.
CHENIN BLANC	Very good	Grows in the Loire Valley, particularly in Vouvray and Saumur.
SAUVIGNON BLANC	Very good	Grows in Sauternes, Graves, and the Loire Valley.
TRAMINER (also called Gewürztraminer)	Very good	Grows in Germany, Alsace, and Italian Tyrol.
COLOMBARD	Fair	Grows in the French commune of Cognac—used for brandy.
FOLLE BLANCHE	Good	Formerly widespread in the commune of Cognac, but is now replaced there by the Ugni Blanc. Does well in the Loire Valley around Nantes as Gros Plant. Called Picpoul in the French Midi, and yields light wine.

THE
WINES
OF
NORTH
AMERICA

When future observers survey the history and development of wine in the United States, I believe they will label the latter half of the twentieth century the dawn of the golden age of American wine. Europe has had two thousand years of experience in the art of making and imbibing wine. The United States, in less than three hundred years, has progressed to the point where it stands on the threshold of a most promising future for both wine production and wine consumption. Today only 17 percent of the wine consumed in the United States is imported.

Up to now, a relatively modest portion of our generous soil has been allocated to the production of wine. So far, twenty-six of our states produce wine commercially (though grapes grow in all fifty), with California far in the lead, producing 70 percent of the wines we drink, the remainder coming principally from New York. But I am sure that the industry's fantastic rate of growth will encourage other states where the climate is propitious to join the ranks of the wine producers.

Perhaps the greatest obstacle in the path of the American winemaker has been his own countrymen's attitude toward his product. Although American wineries now rival all but the very greatest of Europe, native American wines until this past decade lacked statu   and were looked upon with disdain by many wine drinkers, especially in the East.

After Repeal, the only native table wines available were generics of a very low quality. (A generic wine is essentially a combination of a number of different grape varieties, often

The Christian Brothers
Mont La Salle vineyards,
winery, and novitiate

grown in different localities.) These blended wines were, and still are, usually given the names of the famed winemaking areas of Europe (Burgundy, Chablis, Rhine, Sauternes, etc.). Vineyards born overnight hurriedly placed on the market wines made from combinations of grape varieties whose chief virtue lay in their capacity for quick and high yield. These wines, which bore little or no resemblance to those of the areas from which they took their names, had a crude, grapy flavor and were of course no match for the least of the traditional refined European wines, which could now once again be imported.

Then, about 1938, winemakers chose to use basic European grape varieties and attempted to produce less plentiful but better-quality varietals. An American varietal wine such as Pinot Noir or Johannisberg Riesling is named after the specific grape variety employed in its production. A varietal wine is required by law to contain at least 51 percent of the product of the grape from which it takes its name. In order to impart recognizable varietal flavor, good growers generally insist on a higher proportion.

The top California varietals are:

Red	*White*
Cabernet Sauvignon	Pinot Chardonnay
Pinot Noir	Johannisberg Riesling
Zinfandel	Pinot Blanc
Gamay Beaujolais	Chenin Blanc

Since World War II, much progress has been made. Generic wines are now produced in staggering quantities. They have improved with trial and error and, more important, through scientific experimentation. The United States now produces good, uncomplicated, and sturdy everyday wine, often bottled in half-gallon or gallon jugs. Jug wines have attained a great and well-deserved popularity in this country. Most of them cost hardly more, and are certainly better, than the table wine the average Frenchman in Paris or Marseilles drinks every day. Many companies, among them Gallo, Paul Masson, Inglenook, Christian Brothers, and Almadén, are making laudable contributions to American large-scale wine production. In the area of varietals, too, we have made substantial progress, with specialization now becoming the norm.

In New York State and Ohio, a great breakthrough has occurred in the area of hybrids. When in the nineteenth century the phylloxera pest, originally brought to France in the roots of American vines, ravaged the European vines and destroyed most of their vineyards, the French imported American vines that were phylloxera-resistant, grafted their own vines to these healthy roots, and thus saved their vineyards. Later they crossbred the American and European vines, eventually developing a number of hybrids that produced good wines. French-American hybrids are now being used successfully east of the Rockies.

The American consumer's greatest error, once he has taken the step of buying one of our fine native wines, has been his hurry to drink it. No one would dream of purchasing a two-year-old Château Petrus and serving it the same night. Yet many of our best native wines are heedlessly consumed in their infancy, before they have had a chance to develop into what might in many cases be a glorious adulthood. Until 1970, when the California legislature

25

changed the law, even the California vineyard owner was discouraged from aging his wines in his own cellars (thereby doing our job for us) by a yearly inventory tax on all wines held by him on his estate. Luckily, the vintners now will be able to age portions of their vintages without paying tax on the same wine year after year. But let us, the consumers, take the responsibility for giving the better American wines their due by properly aging them in our own cellars or wine racks.

Many of California's finest products are, unfortunately, still too scarce to be available in most parts of the country, but there is hope that this situation may improve in time. Then, too, while in some states, such as California and Illinois, wine may be purchased, as in France, at the grocery store or at the supermarket, in other states, such as Pennsylvania, the sale of all liquor, including wine, is restricted to state-controlled stores. At the present time, although none of our states are totally dry, many townships or counties still are, and in twenty states, including New York, wine may be sold only in private, licensed retail liquor stores.

The men who operate these retail stores have affected and reflected the American wine revolution. Once upon a time, wine was bought in a liquor store from a liquor salesman who happened also to carry some wines, about which he knew little or nothing. Today, wine merchants are students of the subject. The second generation especially—the sons of the men who began or resumed their businesses after Repeal—are becoming more and more knowledgeable about both European and American wines, and many now possess the expertise required to guide their customers.

As more and more Americans are forced by the prohibitively high prices of their favorite French wines to try American wines, the chances are that they will be delighted with what they discover. Americans are beginning to realize that they have a fine native product, much of it suitable for quality everyday drinking. As for our more exalted labels, I predict that there will soon come a day when fine American wine, no longer a poor cousin, will adorn an elegant dinner table anywhere in the world as proudly as any of its distant relatives.

Hand-colored lithograph by Currier and Ives, New York, 1872
The Christian Brothers Collection

Facing: Vintage white wines made from French-American hybrids grown in the Finger Lakes region of New York State

THE VINEYARDS OF CALIFORNIA

The counties of Napa, Sonoma, and Mendocino constitute some of the finest winegrowing regions in the United States, potentially on a par with any of the best vineyard lands of France or Germany. Fine wines grow here for a hundred miles north of the city of San Francisco, on flat valley floors, by swift rivers, on gentle rolling hills, and even on the steep slopes of mountains.

First in importance is the Napa Valley. Strung out on the thread of Highway 29, the "Wine Way" of Napa, are the important wine towns: Calistoga, St. Helena, Rutherford, Oakville, Napa—names that now ring with some of the same authority as those of the famous French wine communes.

The ridge of the Mayacamas Mountains separates Napa from Sonoma County, which in turn runs from the Russian River Valley across to the Pacific. Most of the 13,000 vineyard acres in Sonoma cover the broad, fertile center of the county, from Santa Rosa north through Guerneville, Healdsburg, Asti, and Cloverdale.

Beyond Cloverdale the landscape changes little, even after one enters Mendocino County, the northernmost of the great North Coast wine districts. For many years the inland climate there was thought to be too warm for growing the best wine grapes; now many of the vineyards on cooler hillsides have dramatically proved that Mendocino soil can yield fine fruit from the noble grape varieties.

In the "good old days" before Prohibition, Los Gatos Winery was one small part of the thriving California wine industry

THE VINEYARDS OF CALIFORNIA

Eureka

Ukiah

MENDOCINO AND SONOMA

Sacramento

Santa Rosa

NAPA AND SONOMA

Napa

San Francisco

San Jose

CENTRAL VALLEY

Santa Cruz

Salinas

Monterey

Fresno

SOUTH OF SAN FRANCISCO BAY

Bakersfield

N

W E

S

Los Angeles

PACIFIC OCEAN

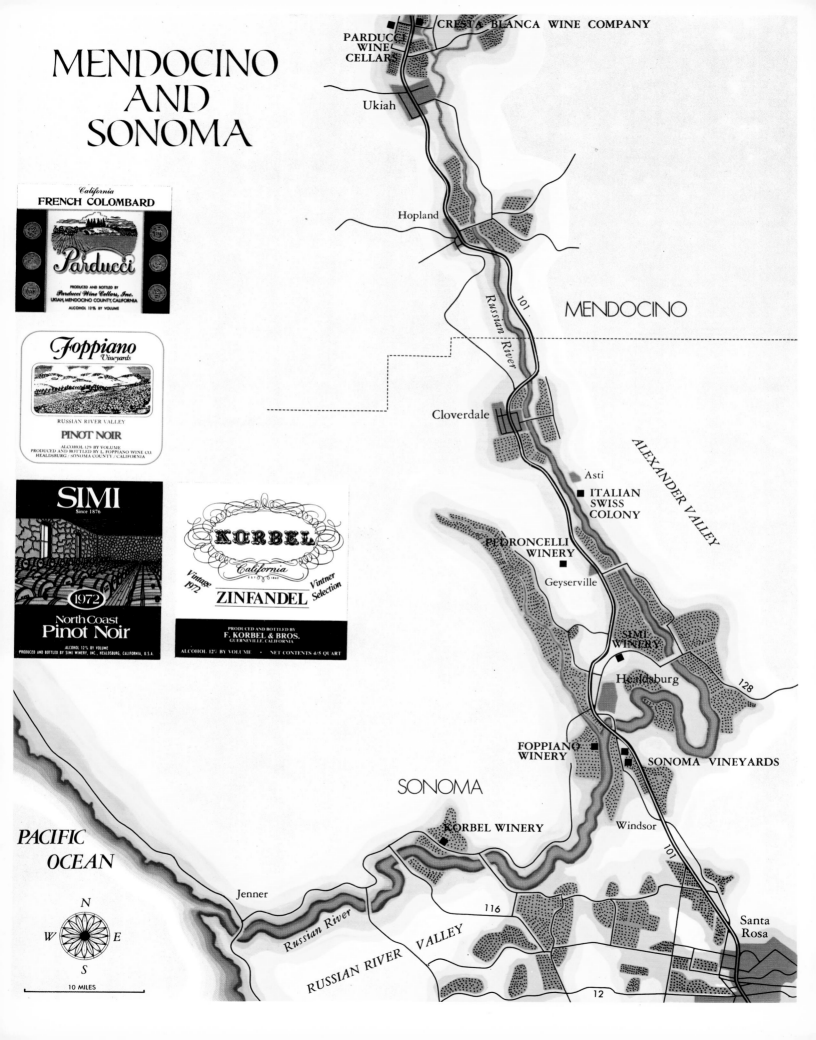

MENDOCINO AND SONOMA

California
FRENCH COLOMBARD

Parducci

PRODUCED AND BOTTLED BY
Parducci Wine Cellars, Inc.
UKIAH, MENDOCINO COUNTY, CALIFORNIA
ALCOHOL 12% BY VOLUME

Foppiano
Vineyards

RUSSIAN RIVER VALLEY
PINOT NOIR

ALCOHOL 12% BY VOLUME
PRODUCED AND BOTTLED BY L. FOPPIANO WINE CO.
HEALDSBURG / SONOMA COUNTY / CALIFORNIA

SIMI
Since 1876

1972

North Coast
Pinot Noir

ALCOHOL 12% BY VOLUME
PRODUCED AND BOTTLED BY SIMI WINERY, INC., HEALDSBURG, CALIFORNIA, U.S.A.

KORBEL
California

Vintage
1972

Vintner
Selection

ZINFANDEL

PRODUCED AND BOTTLED BY
F. KORBEL & BROS.
GUERNEVILLE, CALIFORNIA

ALCOHOL 12% BY VOLUME   •   NET CONTENTS 4/5 QUART

CRESTA BLANCA WINE COMPANY

PARDUCCI
WINE
CELLARS

Ukiah

Hopland

Russian River

101

MENDOCINO

Cloverdale

ALEXANDER VALLEY

Asti
■ **ITALIAN
SWISS
COLONY**

**PEDRONCELLI
WINERY**

Geyserville

**SIMI
WINERY**

Healdsburg

128

**FOPPIANO
WINERY**

SONOMA VINEYARDS

SONOMA

KORBEL WINERY

Windsor

101

**PACIFIC
OCEAN**

Jenner

Russian River

116

Santa
Rosa

RUSSIAN RIVER VALLEY

12

N
W   E
S

10 MILES

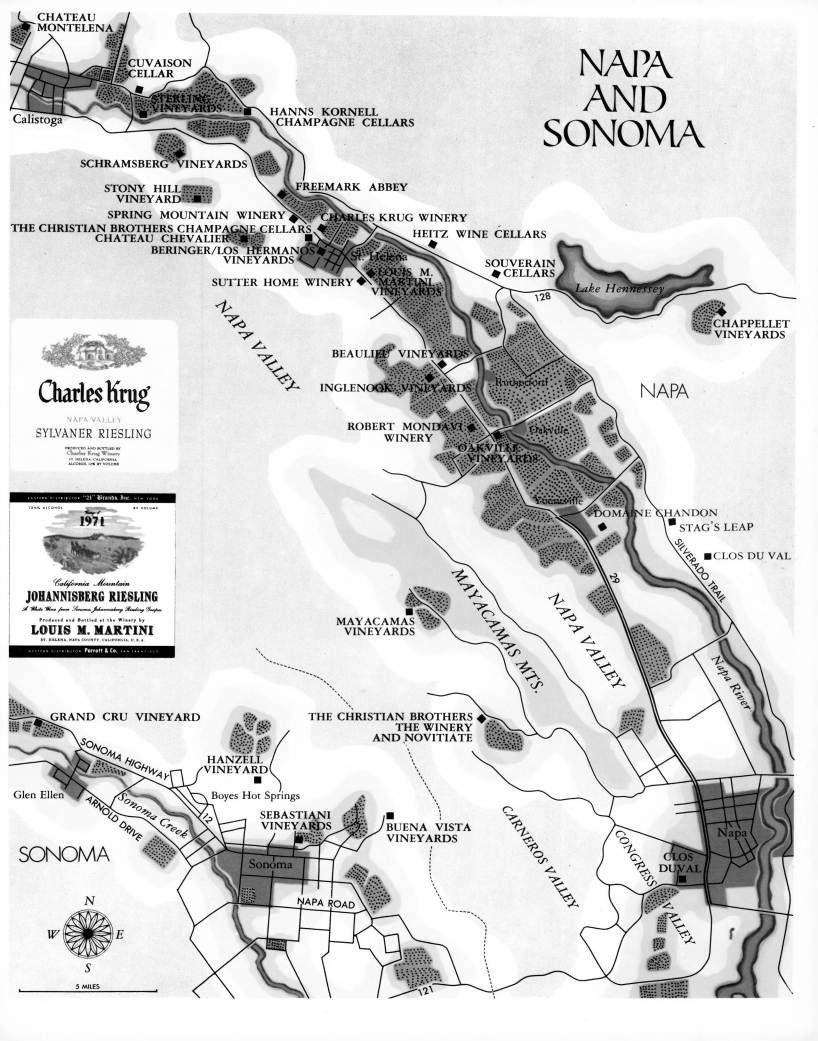

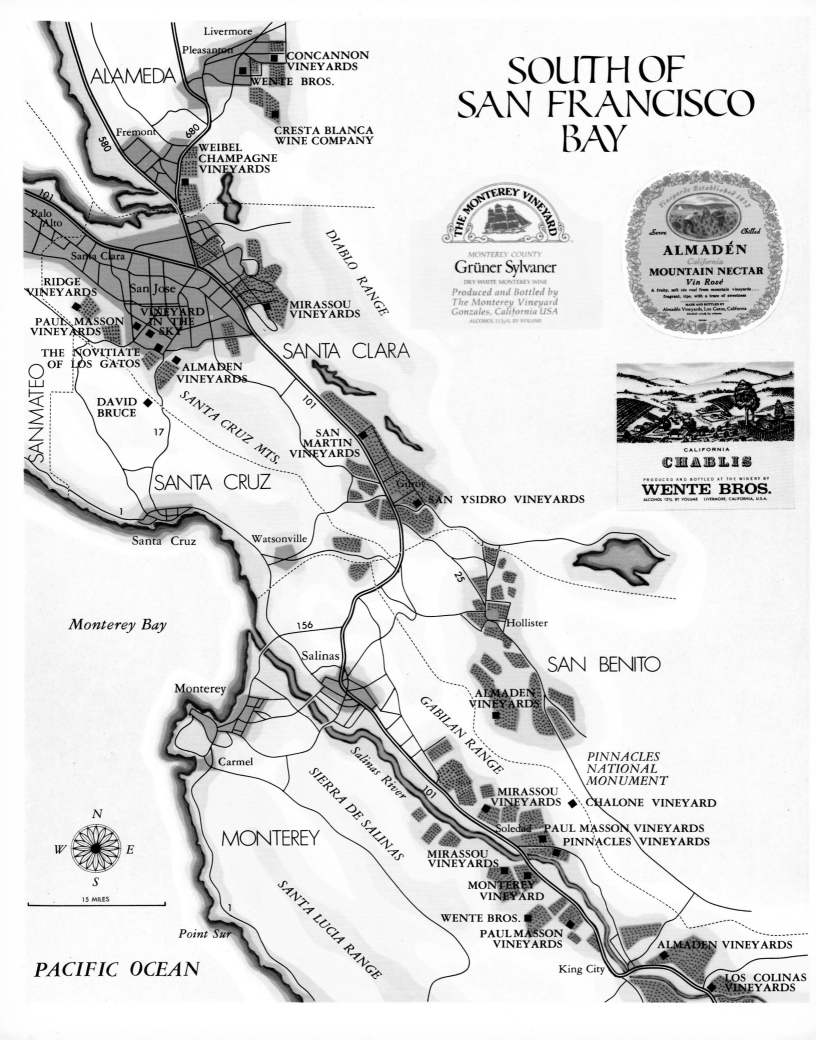

SOUTH OF SAN FRANCISCO BAY

ALAMEDA

Livermore
Pleasanton
Fremont

CONCANNON VINEYARDS
WENTE BROS.
CRESTA BLANCA WINE COMPANY
WEIBEL CHAMPAGNE VINEYARDS

580
680
101

Palo Alto
Santa Clara
San Jose

RIDGE VINEYARDS
PAUL MASSON VINEYARDS
VINEYARD IN THE SKY
THE NOVITIATE OF LOS GATOS
ALMADEN VINEYARDS
DAVID BRUCE

MIRASSOU VINEYARDS

SANTA CLARA

DIABLO RANGE

SAN MATEO

17

SANTA CRUZ MTS.

SANTA CRUZ

101

SAN MARTIN VINEYARDS

Gilroy

SAN YSIDRO VINEYARDS

1
Santa Cruz
Watsonville

Monterey Bay

156
25

Salinas
Hollister

SAN BENITO

Monterey
Carmel

SIERRA DE SALINAS

Salinas River

GABILAN RANGE

ALMADEN VINEYARDS

PINNACLES NATIONAL MONUMENT

MONTEREY

101

MIRASSOU VINEYARDS
CHALONE VINEYARD

Soledad

PAUL MASSON VINEYARDS
PINNACLES VINEYARDS

MIRASSOU VINEYARDS

MONTEREY VINEYARD

WENTE BROS.

PAUL MASSON VINEYARDS

King City

ALMADEN VINEYARDS

LOS COLINAS VINEYARDS

SANTA LUCIA RANGE

1
Point Sur

PACIFIC OCEAN

N W E S

15 MILES

---

label: THE MONTEREY VINEYARD ™
MONTEREY COUNTY
Grüner Sylvaner
DRY WHITE MONTEREY WINE
Produced and Bottled by
The Monterey Vineyard
Gonzales, California USA
ALCOHOL 11½% BY VOLUME

label: Vineyards Established 1852
Serve Chilled
ALMADÉN
California
MOUNTAIN NECTAR
Vin Rosé
A fruity, soft vin rosé from mountain vineyards...
fragrant, ripe, with a trace of sweetness
MADE AND BOTTLED BY
Almadén Vineyards, Los Gatos, California
Alcohol 11½% by volume

label: CALIFORNIA
CHABLIS
PRODUCED AND BOTTLED AT THE WINERY BY
WENTE BROS.
ALCOHOL 12% BY VOLUME   LIVERMORE, CALIFORNIA, U.S.A.

The Livermore Valley, an hour's drive south of San Francisco, has gained renown for its white wines and boasts two famed wineries: Concannon and Wente Bros. Concannon is still expanding its vineyards in Livermore, while Wente Bros. has planted several hundred acres in Monterey County.

Under the guidance of Franciscan fathers, who cultivated grapes there as far back as 1777, Santa Clara was the first of the northern California districts to be planted with the vine. Both Paul Masson and Almadén retain their historic homes and central winery operations here, while planting vast acreages of vines farther to the south, in Monterey and San Benito counties. Much of the movement southward was inspired by research at the University of California at Davis; Professors Maynard Amerine and Albert Winkler proved that the proximity of the sea and the movement of cool air between the mountains in this neglected area can produce a temperature that will permit superior varietal grapes to flourish.

California's midsection is a remarkably fertile trough lying between the coastal mountains and the higher Sierra ranges to the east. The central valleys, the Sacramento in the north and the San Joaquin in the south, join to create one of the most productive agricultural areas on earth, where water transported from mountain reservoirs greens thousands of previously parched areas. The San Joaquin Valley alone counts more than 700 square miles under vine. But of course not all of this immense vineyard is devoted exclusively to table-wine grapes; San Joaquin supplies the nation with all its raisins and nearly all its domestic brandy. The valley grows half of all the wine made in the United States.

Yet here, as elsewhere, tremendous yields mean wines of less than exceptional quality. Vines of the Central Valley bear second-rate grapes for table wines but first-rate grapes for fortified wines and brandies. Though the grapes may not be the best for making great wines, the standards of the giant wineries are as high and exacting as any in the state. The goals are, of course, different at the high-volume producers, yet their expertise and awareness of the most modern viticultural techniques are second to none.

Almost unbelievable quantities of jug wine, or *vin ordinaire*, tell the story of wine in the Central Valley. The wineries that make it are among the largest in the world. Wine drinkers are grateful for the existence of the Central Valley, just as people in France are happy about the fact that there is a Midi, the source of much of the everyday wine of that country.

More and more small wineries, some of which have already established reputations for excellence, are springing up in California. Most choose to specialize in two or three premium varietals such as Cabernet Sauvignon, Zinfandel, Chardonnay, Johannisberg Riesling. Quantities are so limited that many wineries sell out the vintage by the time it is bottled. Few are available outside California, but here are some names to look for: Hacienda, Carneros Creek, Burgess, Kenwood, Château St. Jean, Joseph Phelps, Mt. Veeder, and Joseph Swan.

On the pages that follow we describe our personal favorites among the many fine vineyards of California and make recommendations for specific wines from each source. Since many of our choices represent wines with limited production and distribution, the selection—and approximate prices—may vary from one section of the state to another. None of the recommendations carry a vintage date. For comments on which years to seek out and which to avoid, see A Chart of Recent Vintage Years, page 156.

HOW TO READ A CALIFORNIA WINE LABEL

Wine labels present a great deal of information that is both useful and instructive. In the case of California wines, state and federal laws require that the label state a number of facts about the contents of the bottle. Listed below are some of the elements to look for on a California wine label.

Produced and bottled by
To earn the right to use the word "produced" the winery must by law ferment and mature at least 75 percent of the wine in the bottle.

Made and bottled by
A much less exact phrase, meaning that at least 10 percent (a small fraction indeed) of the wine in the bottle was vinified and aged at the winery.

Cellared and bottled by, Prepared and bottled by, Blended and bottled by
Vague and loosely applied phrases. It can be assumed that wine so labeled was *produced* by someone other than the bottler. Certain cellar operations might be involved, but the quality of the wine is dependent on the unnamed vintner who shipped the wine to the bottler.

Selected and bottled by
Same as above, but no added cellar operations were performed.

Bottled at the winery
The wine was bottled on the premises where it was produced or where it was blended and finished.

Vintage date
No less than 95 percent of the wine contained in the bottle was fermented from grapes grown and harvested in the year stated. In addition, the grapes must have been grown exclusively in the district mentioned on the bottle. The remaining 5 percent of the contents is legally permitted to be wine from another year. (This is a wise

and practical measure, allowing for the "topping" of casks to replace wine lost through normal evaporation or leakage.) The date alone, not preceded by the word "vintage," means only that the wine was bottled in the year stated.

The appellation "California"

The wine is made entirely from grapes grown, and their juice fermented, in California. If any part of the finished product contains any wine from grapes grown outside the state, it may not be labeled "California." (This rigid regulation is not true in New York or Ohio.) Nor can sugar be added unless it is exclusively derived from the grape.

District appellation

If the wine label gives a county or district name, 75 percent of the grapes must have been grown in the region specified. Thus a "Napa Valley" wine is legally required to contain 75 percent of Napa grapes.

Estate-bottled

Only wine bottled on the estate where the grapes were grown and in a winery under the same ownership is entitled to be labeled "estate-bottled." Like château bottling in Bordeaux, this guarantees authenticity but not necessarily high quality.

Varietal wines

A varietal wine is one named after the grape variety from which it is produced and having the predominant taste and aroma characteristic of the variety. At least 51 percent of its volume must be derived from that grape—for example, Pinot Noir, Zinfandel, Chardonnay, etc. In practice, the better vineyards use a much higher percentage of the grape than is required by law in order to give the wine more of the characteristic of the grape variety on the label.

Generic wines

A generic wine is a blend of many different grape varieties and usually carries a name such as Burgundy, Sauterne, or Chablis. The practice of using European place names for generic wines started in the United States in the nineteenth century and still persists. But it is hoped that we will develop our own place names for generic wines in the future.

Proprietary wines

A proprietary wine is a blended wine for which the winery has created an attractive fantasy name (Emerald Dry, for example) which will help sell the product. Usually the proprietary wines are secret blends with their own distinctive characteristics; they range from average to very high quality.

Bottle-fermented champagne

The sparkle is the result of a natural process of fermentation acting on the wine within a closed container.

Charmat-process (or bulk-process) champagne

The sparkle is the result of a secondary fermentation that took place in a glass-lined tank or vat instead of a bottle. In either case the container is tightly sealed during the secondary fermentation to prevent the carbon dioxide bubbles from escaping.

35

NAPA VALLEY GAMAY 1972

At least 75 percent of the grapes come from the region; at least 51 percent of the wine from the Gamay. "Produced and bottled by" guarantees at least 75 percent of the contents was fermented and matured at the Mondavi winery.

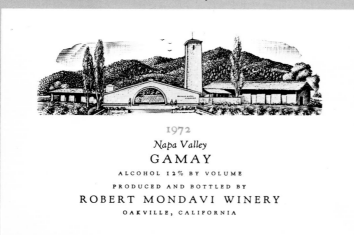

1972
Napa Valley
GAMAY
ALCOHOL 12% BY VOLUME
PRODUCED AND BOTTLED BY
ROBERT MONDAVI WINERY
OAKVILLE, CALIFORNIA

THE BEST RED WINE GRAPE OF CALIFORNIA

Since no vintage year appears, it can be assumed that the wine is a blend of vintages, ready for drinking now.

the
Christian Brothers®
VINTNERS SINCE 1882

SELECT NAPA VALLEY
CABERNET SAUVIGNON
A dry red wine of great character and finesse
PRODUCED AND BOTTLED BY
THE CHRISTIAN BROTHERS • NAPA, CALIFORNIA
Alcohol 12% by volume

RIDGE
CALIFORNIA
PETITE SIRAH
YORK CREEK
1971

GRAPES FROM SPRING MOUNTAIN, NAPA COUNTY
BOTTLED APR 1973 ALCOHOL 13.4% BY VOLUME
PRODUCED AND BOTTLED BY RIDGE VINEYARDS
17100 MONTE BELLO RD, CUPERTINO, CALIFORNIA

A WINE FROM ONE SPECIFIC PLOT

Many fine vintners add the name of the section of vines which produced the wine. Here the key phrase is "York Creek."

Vineyards Established 1852
Serve   *Chilled*

ALMADÉN
California Mountain
GRENACHE ROSÉ
A fresh, appetizing fragrant rosé wine
made from the famous Grenache grape of France
grown in California vineyards
MADE AND BOTTLED BY
Almadén Vineyards, Los Gatos, California
Alcohol 12½% by volume
22556A

OUR LEADING VIN ROSÉ

The varietal grape Grenache, which makes the celebrated pink wine of Tavel in France, also flourishes in California.

POPULAR PROPRIETARY NAMES

California viticulturalists developed the Emerald Riesling grape, a hybrid of the German Johannisberg Riesling. Employing this grape, Paul Masson produced a wine with its own registered proprietary name.

THE GREAT GRAPE OF WHITE BURGUNDY WINE

The first-rate grape and the simple, precise phrases on the label speak well for the quality of the wine. Vineyard name, vintage date, valley name, and varietal grape name constitute the classic labeling formula for all great California wines.

AMERICA'S MOST POPULAR RED WINE

"California" tells us all the wine was grown in that state. "Made and bottled at" attests that at least 10 percent of the wine was vinified at the winery. "Burgundy" is a blend of grapes.

WHAT DOES CHÂTEAU MEAN IN CALIFORNIA?

"Château" is an elegant word with no technical meaning. Wente has blended two superior varietals, Sémillon and Sauvignon Blanc, the grapes that give us the Sauternes of France.

BEAULIEU VINEYARDS

Rutherford, Napa County

Fine traditions stand behind many of the important Napa Valley wineries; some are longer but none grander than the story of the great men and remarkable wines associated with the handsome place that is Beaulieu.

Until 1973 the man who made the Cabernet Sauvignons and Pinot Noirs and all the other Beaulieu wines was the dedicated André Tchelistcheff, brought to the vineyard in 1938 by its founder, Georges de Latour. Tchelistcheff's European vinicultural training and de Latour's ties to Bordeaux and Burgundy ensured the traditionally high quality of the wines. Their successors do their work well.

Beringer's Johannisberg Riesling

RECOMMENDED WINES

Red

Burgundy	about $3
Beaumont Pinot Noir	about $5
Private Reserve Cabernet Sauvignon	over $8

White

Beaufort Pinot Chardonnay	about $5

Sparkling

B.V. Brut	about $5

hopes are geared to placing Beringer wines once again among the best in the valley.

RECOMMENDED WINES

White

Fumé Blanc	about $3
Johannisberg Riesling	about $3

BERINGER

St. Helena, Napa County.

The Beringer brothers came from Germany and in 1876 built a homestead at St. Helena. It was the oldest family-owned winery in the Napa Valley when the Swiss Nestlé Corporation acquired the 700-acre vineyard in 1970. The new owners have installed the best modern winery equipment and hired an enthusiastic, skilled winemaker and enologist—Myron Nightingale—to take charge of the vintages. Their efforts and

CHÂTEAU MONTELENA

Napa, Calistoga County

In the few short years since its purchase by Lee Pashich in 1968, Château Montelena has made a remarkable name for itself. At an early 1976 tasting, French connoisseurs hailed the 1973 Chardonnay as a better wine than a number of illustrious white Burgundies. Similar praise may be expected from Bordeaux wine authorities when Château Montelena's Cabernet Sauvignons are ready for drinking.

Château Montelena follows a familiar Napa Valley pattern—an old 19th-century winery refitted with the most modern European and American winemaking equipment, supplied by vineyards growing only a few choice vinifera varieties. The formula works well, and we look forward to tasting more wines from this talented producer as they mature in the years ahead.

RECOMMENDED WINES

Red
Cabernet Sauvignon   about $9

White
Chardonnay   about $7

BUENA VISTA
Sonoma, Sonoma County
Count Agoston Haraszthy, a political exile from Hungary, founded the Buena Vista vineyard in 1856, and became known as the father of modern California winemaking. In 1943, Frank Bartholomew, then the Chairman of the Board of United Press International, acquired the long-neglected Buena Vista vineyard.

During the 1960s, wine connoisseurs sought out Bartholomew's cask-numbered Cabernet Sauvignon, Chardonnay, Green Hungarian, and his remarkable Zinfandel. Buena Vista was sold in 1968 to Vernon Underwood of Young's Market Company of Los Angeles, the Bartholomews retaining their home and a small adjoining vineyard, where fine wine is still made.

RECOMMENDED WINE

Red
Zinfandel   about $3

FREEMARK ABBEY
St. Helena, Napa County
At this vineyard was born the fabulous Pinot Chardonnay that outclassed the best

Barrel-cleaning tools, Freemark Abbey

of the Corton Charlemagnes and Montrachets offered in a blind tasting held with European and American wine experts in 1974.

Not long ago Freemark Abbey was one of the tiny "boutique" producers. Now it boasts an annual production of 20,000 cases—almost the size of Lafite-Rothschild.

RECOMMENDED WINES

Red
Cabernet Sauvignon   about $8
Cabernet Bosché   over $8

White
Johannisberg Riesling   about $5
Pinot Chardonnay   over $8

CUVAISON, INC.
Calistoga, Napa County
Interesting small innovative vineyards now dot the best vine-growing region of northern California, reminiscent of the little vine patches one finds in Burgundy and Bor-

deaux, homes of some of the finest wines in the world.

One of the tiny "boutique" vineyards is Cuvaison, started by Thomas Cottrell and Thomas Parkhill—a scientist and an electrical engineer. Philip Togni, formerly of Chappellet, is now the winemaker for the new owners, a New York corporation called CT. The wines are pleasant and authentic and can be excellent values.

RECOMMENDED WINES

White
Chenin Blanc	about $3
Pinot Chardonnay	about $5

CHAPPELLET
St. Helena, Napa County
Donn Chappellet, heir to part of the Lockheed fortune, in 1969 left his luxurious home in Beverly Hills for the rugged life of mountain climbing and winegrowing. In a few short years he and his family have extracted from the soil a Cabernet Sauvignon

Chappellet vineyard, overlooking Napa Valley

that is sought after. There is also a Chenin Blanc that some consider the best of its kind in California, as well as a quite remarkable Johannisberg Riesling.

RECOMMENDED WINES

Red
Cabernet Sauvignon	about $8

White
Chenin Blanc	under $5
Johannisberg Riesling	about $5

THE CHRISTIAN BROTHERS
Napa County
The Christian Brothers are a Catholic teaching order founded in 1680 in the Champagne district of France by Saint Jean Baptiste de la Salle. The proceeds of their winemaking help support nearly two hundred schools and colleges, including St. Mary's College in the San Francisco East Bay and Manhattan College in New York.

In 1882 the Christian Brothers started to make sacramental wine in California for their own use; their wines became available to the public in the 1930s and are now distributed by Fromm and Sichel. It is important to know that they make their wine in such a way that it is ready to drink when it reaches the wine merchant's shelf.

RECOMMENDED WINES

Red
Cabernet Sauvignon	under $5
Brother Timothy Zinfandel	under $5

White
Chenin Blanc	under $3
Napa Fumé	under $5

CLOS DU VAL

Yountville, Napa County

The noblest of Bordeaux winemaking traditions were transferred to the Napa Valley when Bernard Portet, son of the manager of the wines at Château Lafite-Rothschild, chose not to work with his father. He now seeks his fortune along the Silverado Trail, at Clos du Val.

Lafite-Rothschild stresses the Cabernet Sauvignon combined with the Merlot grape. Clos du Val does the same in Napa. Merlot contributes softness and light elegance, while Cabernet Sauvignon offers depth and long life. The first of the Clos du Val wines, which strove to capture the essence of the Haut-Médoc, reached the American market early in 1975. Since fine red wines like these need five to ten years in the bottle, we will not know for certain until the next decade if this vineyard—soon to produce 13,000 cases a year—has brought the qualities of Pauillac to Napa. Clos du Val certainly bears watching.

RECOMMENDED WINES

Red

Cabernet Sauvignon	about $5
Zinfandel	over $5

FOPPIANO

Healdsburg, Sonoma County

Since 1896 the Foppiano family has been growing grapes and making wine not far from the Russian River in central Sonoma County, with the emphasis on rich, barrel-wood character for its hearty reds. Much of the vineyard acreage has recently been replanted to bring the selection of vines into line with contemporary viticultural ideas. However, the huge, old-fashioned redwood aging tanks remain an integral part of the Foppiano operation.

RECOMMENDED WINES

Red

Pinot Noir	under $5

White

Chenin Blanc	about $3

GRAND CRU

Glen Ellen, Sonoma County

After years of dormancy, in 1971 the pleasant stone winery (formerly called Sonoma County Winery) sprang to life again under the new name Grand Cru. Allen Ferrara and Robert Magnani are the pair responsible for the magical comeback.

The wines to try are the three Zinfandels. The reds are typically rich and full, the equal of any in the state; the rosé is darker and deeper in flavor than the pink wines made by the other important California wineries; most interesting of the distinguished output is the white called Zinfandel Blanc de Noir, a light, fresh, fruity wine, expensive but well worth searching out. Scarcely half a dozen wineries in the state make a white Zinfandel, and the one from Grand Cru is probably the best.

RECOMMENDED WINE

Red

Zinfandel	under $5

INGLENOOK

Rutherford, Napa County

With a hundred years of tradition and many fine wines behind it, Inglenook commands respect and admiration from the other major vintners in the valley. Now owned by the large Heublein Corporation through their subsidiary United Vintners, Inglenook is able to distribute widely its extensive range of wines.

41

RECOMMENDED WINES

Red

Pinot Noir	about $5
Cabernet Sauvignon Cask	under $8

White

Johannisberg Riesling	about $4
Sauvignon Blanc	about $4
Gewürztraminer	about $4

HEITZ CELLARS

St. Helena, Napa County

One of the most idealistic of winemakers is Joe Heitz, a former schoolteacher who became a legend not long after his 1960 graduation from Davis. The Heitz magic touch turns good purchased grapes into great wines, but Heitz also has vines of his own, and he often gives his bottles specific location designations indicating which part of the vineyard the grapes come from.

Joe Heitz's wines typically have much richness and depth, especially the Pinot Chardonnays and Cabernet Sauvignons. He makes some of the finest generic bottlings

Barrels of wine aging in Heitz Cellars

Facing: Tasting room at Inglenook, built in 1887

in California, and these are less expensive than his varietals.

RECOMMENDED WINES

Red

Barbera	about $5
Cabernet Sauvignon	about $8

White

Gewürztraminer	about $5
Pinot Chardonnay	over $8

ITALIAN SWISS COLONY

Asti, Sonoma County

The two best-known nationally advertised brands in California jug wines are Gallo and Italian Swiss Colony. Gallo's headquarters are in the Central Valley, but Italian Swiss clings to its historic roots in Asti, far up in Sonoma County. Gallo remains family-owned, but Italian Swiss Colony is part of United Vintners, the same company that owns the Beaulieu and Inglenook vineyards.

The fact that Italian Swiss Colony is in Sonoma does not mean that all their grapes are grown there. Many come from the Central Valley, where yields are higher and costs considerably lower. The firm now owns several large wineries in the valley. Though Italian Swiss Colony does not set out to make wine of the distinction of many of its Sonoma neighbors', one cannot deny the important contribution to American wines of this giant organization.

RECOMMENDED WINE

Red

Zinfandel	under $3

KORBEL

Guerneville, Sonoma County

For nearly a century Korbel champagnes

43

Pruning vines on a frosty morning, Korbel's vineyard

Wines fermenting in refrigerated tanks at Robert Mondavi

have been made on the banks of the Russian River in the center of Sonoma County. True fame came only with a consumers' report that pronounced Korbel the best United States champagne. Volume tripled virtually overnight and Korbel Brut became so desirable that it had to be rationed.

Korbel Natural, a wine born in much uncertainty, has become one of the firm's most famous products. It gets its name from the fact that practically no sugar is added to the wine after the sediment is disgorged.

Since 1965, Korbel has produced still table wines, including Grey Riesling, Chenin Blanc, Pinot Noir, and Cabernet Sauvignon. Though good, none of these approaches the excellence of Korbel sparkling wines.

RECOMMENDED WINES

Sparkling
Brut   about $5
Natural   under $8

ROBERT MONDAVI
Oakville, Napa County

Robert Mondavi's Cabernet Sauvignon is often served at the White House and at dinners given by the State Department. This stamp of approval and the accompanying publicity have made it the single most sought-after red wine of the Western Hemisphere.

Robert Mondavi's wines represent a lifetime of hard work, long hours, and constant dedication.

RECOMMENDED WINES

Red
California Table Wine   under $3
Cabernet Sauvignon   under $8

White
California Table Wine   under $3
Pinot Chardonnay   about $5
Fumé Blanc   about $5

Rosé
Gamay   under $3

THE PEDRONCELLI WINERY
Geyserville, Sonoma County

In 1927 John Pedroncelli planted a hillside vineyard and built a small wine cellar just outside Geyserville. Today his two sons, John and James, have expanded the original 60-acre vineyard to almost twice that size, producing about 150,000 gallons of wine a year. Their Zinfandel Rosé was a California first, and several of their wines consistently win medals at state fairs. Their Sonoma County Red represents the best quality for the price in bulk wines.

.RECOMMENDED WINES

Red

Sonoma County	half-gallon about $4
Gamay Beaujolais	about $3–$4
Pinot Noir	about $5

White

Sonoma County	half-gallon about $4

The San Francisco Ballet performing at Sonoma Vineyards

SONOMA VINEYARDS
Windsor, Sonoma County

Rodney D. Strong now rules one of the largest domains of estate-bottled superior-grade varieties in all California.

Sonoma's plantings are limited to the leading four grape varieties: Cabernet Sauvignon, Chardonnay., Johannisberg Riesling, and Pinot Noir. At some point Merlot will be added to provide softness, as is done in Bordeaux.

Perhaps Strong's most creative contribution is his concept of a specific vineyard label rather than one simply bearing the valley name of Sonoma. The label will read "Sonoma County, Iron Horse Vineyard, Pinot Noir 1975, estate-bottled by Sonoma Vineyards."

Below this level, but still estate-bottled, will be the same varietals. However, the specific vineyard name will not be mentioned and the cost will be somewhat lower.

RECOMMENDED WINES

Red

Zinfandel	about $3

White

Summer Riesling	under $3
Johannisberg Riesling	about $5

Sparkling

Brut	under $8

HANNS KORNELL
St. Helena, Napa County

Hanns Kornell has established his name as one of the greatest champagne makers in America. Kornell makes wine under his own label as well as for many vintners in Napa who have neither the facilities nor the patience to make their own. His raw materials—the still wines he blesses with bubbles—are purchased from friends

45

throughout the valley. All Kornell wines are fermented in the bottle and disgorged in the traditional manner.

RECOMMENDED WINES

Sparkling
Extra Dry	under $8
Sehr Trocken	about $8

CHARLES KRUG
St. Helena, Napa County

Two great families remain active in Napa: one at Louis M. Martini, the other at Charles Krug. In love with the land and wine of northern California, Cesare Mondavi bought the Charles Krug estate as a place to make wine and to bring up his children. One son, Robert, left the fold to found his own business. The other son, Peter, now manages Charles Krug.

Charles Krug makes an especially fine Cabernet Sauvignon, some of the greatest vintages dating from the 1950s. The more recent bottles will generously repay a decade of cool rest in a dark cellar. Charles Krug white wines may not require the same at-home aging, but the rewards are just as great.

RECOMMENDED WINES

Red
Cabernet Sauvignon	about $5

White
Pinot Chardonnay	under $5
Gewürztraminer	under $5

OAKVILLE VINEYARDS
Oakville, Napa County

Oakville, revived and refurbished a few years ago by a group of partners, produced some fine wines that appeared to hold great promise for the future. In 1976, the winery and vineyard holdings were sold to the Heublein corporation, which owns the adjacent property of Inglenook. The wine inventory, however—some 30,000 cases and 144,000 gallons in bulk—and the Oakville label were bought by Robert Mondavi, the only other winery in the town of Oakville. Mondavi plans to continue the label. The wines still available are well worth buying.

RECOMMENDED WINES

Red
Cabernet Sauvignon	under $8

White
Our House	under $3
Johannisberg Riesling	under $5
Sauvignon Blanc	about $5

HANZELL
Sonoma, Sonoma County

The late J. D. Zellerbach, former United States Ambassador to Italy, was a lover of great Burgundy wines. His dream was to reproduce on a smaller scale, in the Sonoma hills of California, the great château of the Clos de Vougeot in Burgundy, and to make there a Pinot Chardonnay rivaling Montrachet and a Pinot Noir approaching the quality of Clos de Vougeot.

Whether or not his noble red and superb white match their French counterparts is a matter of much discussion. Tasters agree that the white wine stands up to a big white Burgundy, but most would say that the Pinot Noir has not yet fulfilled the dream.

In 1963, this valuable and beautiful wine property was acquired by Douglas and Mary Day. Under their aegis quality continued to improve. Hanzell is now managed with equal care by their daughter and son-in-law. With each passing year the taste approaches closer and closer to Montrachet and Clos de Vougeot. It is hoped that their wines will ultimately become classics in the annals of California winegrowing.

RECOMMENDED WINES

Red

Pinot Noir	about $8

White

Pinot Chardonnay	about $8

SOUVERAIN CELLARS
Alexander Valley, Sonoma County

RUTHERFORD HILL WINERY
Rutherford, Napa Valley
Souverain Cellars, a subsidiary of the Pillsbury Company, consisted of two wineries, the larger, Souverain of Alexander Valley in Sonoma County, and the original Souverain of Rutherford in Napa Valley.

In 1976 Pillsbury sold Souverain of Alexander Valley and the Souverain name to a cooperative known as North Coast Cellars. The winery is capable of producing 2 million gallons. The winery in Napa was sold to another group, headed by Charles Carpy and William Jaeger, part owners of Freemark Abbey. In the past the wines were vintage varietals from Napa Valley, both whites and reds distinguished by their soft style. Under the new name of Rutherford Hill Winery the owners expect eventually to produce 50,000 cases a year, but no significant quantities of wine will appear until 1978.

RECOMMENDED WINES

Red

Zinfandel	under $5
Cabernet Sauvignon	under $8

STONY HILL
Napa, Napa County
Obtaining a case of Pinot Chardonnay from Fred and Eleanor McCrea is one of the great West Coast adventures. For those who care, it is worth whatever effort or cost is entailed. The following plan should reward you with twelve bottles of the famous Stony Hill wine: (1) live in California; (2) be on the McCrea mailing list; (3) once notified that the wine is ready, get up to the vineyard within two weeks (or your reservation will expire and some other eager wine lover will have carted off your Chardonnay or Johannisberg Riesling).

RECOMMENDED WINES

White

Johannisberg Riesling	under $8
Pinot Chardonnay	about $8

SPRING MOUNTAIN
St. Helena, Napa County
There is a handsome hundred-year-old Victorian house near St. Helena with vines in front and a winery in its cellar. Michael Robbins, a lawyer and engineer from Iowa, went on a business trip to Napa Valley in 1963, saw the charming structure, and could not resist acquiring it.

In 1970 Robbins let the world taste his Cabernet Sauvignon, Chardonnay, and Sauvignon Blanc. His 85 acres have been saluted by the San Francisco wine community as utterly remarkable and their wines as equal to the best of these three varietals produced by any other Napa Valley vineyard. Off to an auspicious start, Robbins may in time make wine history.

RECOMMENDED WINES

Red

Cabernet Sauvignon	over $8

White

Sauvignon Blanc	about $5
Pinot Chardonnay	over $8

47

STERLING
Calistoga, Napa County
Perched on a ridge high over northern Napa Valley, Sterling plans ultimately to produce 100,000 cases a year.

We have tasted many of their wines, and some have already proved astonishing. Both the Pinot Chardonnay and the Sauvignon Blanc are excellent, but the true glories from Sterling are the reds. Seventy percent of the vineyard is planted in Cabernet Sauvignon and Merlot, the two grapes basic to great red Bordeaux. Though understandably less elegant, the Zinfandel, too, shows fine bouquet and body.

RECOMMENDED WINES

Red
Cabernet Sauvignon   under $8

White
Chenin Blanc   about $5
Chardonnay   about $7

MAYACAMAS
Napa, Napa County
Bob Travers studied with and was inspired by Joe Heitz of Napa. In 1968 the Travers family moved to a 2,400-foot-high slope in the Mayacamas Mountains on the site of an extinct volcano.

The 40 acres of land were planted exclusively with superior varieties—Chardonnay and Cabernet Sauvignon. Plans include eventually doubling the acreage. The total present production is about 7,000 cases, much of it allocated to friends in the San Francisco area, leaving only a token quantity for sale in prestigious shops across the rest of the country. The most talked-about of all the Mayacamas wines is the Late Harvest Zinfandel of 1968, one of the most concentrated wines ever produced in California. The natural alcohol in this wine reaches an astonishing 17 percent, and the power is reflected on the palate.

The vineyard is well on its way to being a 20th-century phenomenon. High mountains result in low-yield grapes and high labor costs, so the wine commands high prices.

RECOMMENDED WINES

Red
Cabernet Sauvignon   over $8
Zinfandel   over $8

White
Pinot Chardonnay   over $8

DOMAINE CHANDON
Yountville, Napa County
The great French firm of Moët-Hennessey, makers of some of the finest French champagnes and cognacs, established its American company, Domaine Chandon, in Napa Valley in 1973. Recognizing the potential for good sparkling wines made from grapes grown in California, they have built at Yountville a large facility that will eventually produce 120,000 cases under the Chandon label. Using the traditional French method, the firm will, according to president John Wright, be striving for delicacy with depth. Domaine Chandon produces two cuvées: Napa Valley Brut and Cuvée de Pinot Noir (which is made with 100 percent Pinot Noir). Both are vinified extremely dry. Champagne master Edmund Maudière comes over from Epernay to supervise the blending of the wines and he oversees other steps in production. The wines are somewhat similar in style to their French counterpart—rather dry, with delicate fruit; the blend incorporates more Pinot Blanc and Pinot Noir than Chardonnay, which Maudière feels is too rich. Chandon wines are not vintage-dated be-

cause of California law, which requires that 95 percent of a given vintage be used in the wine. Like the parent company in France, Chandon uses older wines in the blends for added depth and character.

RECOMMENDED WINES

Sparkling

Napa Valley Brut	about $8
Cuvée de Pinot Noir	about $8

STAG'S LEAP WINE CELLARS
Napa, Napa County

Stag's Leap, a new and tiny winery located at the southeastern end of Napa Valley, startled the wine world in mid-1976 by winning first place with its Cabernet Sauvignon in a blind tasting in Paris. Competing against top classified growths of the Médoc, including the illustrious Château Mouton-Rothschild, this 1973 Cabernet Sauvignon received the highest number of points awarded at the tasting, which was conducted by some of France's leading wine experts. Owned by Warren Winiarski, formerly on the faculty of the University of Chicago, the winery also makes Johannisberg Riesling and Gamay. Production is small, so that the wines are scarce and command respectable prices, which, if you can find them, they are well worth.

RECOMMENDED WINES

Red

Cabernet Sauvignon	about $8

White

Johannisberg Riesling	about $6

SUTTER HOME
St. Helena, Napa County

The Sutter Home Winery was built in 1874 by John Sutter, of gold discovery fame. Since World War II the property has been the pride of the Trinchero family. Their Zinfandel 1968 is fondly remembered, as are some of its worthy successors.

Most of Sutter Home Zinfandel grapes grow in the Sierra foothills of Amador County, east of Sacramento. They yield a wine that is tannic, rich, and long-lived. Look for labels with specific designations such as Deaver Vineyard Zinfandel. Extended bottle life is one of the great attributes of Sutter Home Zinfandel; longevity is unusual for wines made from that grape.

RECOMMENDED WINE

Red

Zinfandel	under $5

YVERDON
Spring Mountain, Napa County

Fred and Russell Aves have created, literally with their own hands, a handsome winery high on Spring Mountain. The 90 acres of vineyards are planted exclusively with very good grape varieties: Chardonnay, Pinot Noir, and Johannisberg Riesling. The first vintage (1971) and the harvests that followed produced some lovely wines which should grow and improve in the future.

RECOMMENDED WINES

Red

Gamay Beaujolais	under $5
Cabernet Sauvignon	under $8

LOUIS M. MARTINI
St. Helena, Napa County

By latest count, twenty-two large corporations have attempted to buy this great vineyard. The wines from the family's thousand acres in Napa and Sonoma have long set a standard of reliability and excellence. Some say the Pinot Noir does not thrive in California, but upon tasting the Louis Martini version, many wine experts have shown new respect. The Cabernet Sauvignon and Gewürztraminer are models of their types. The Italian-style Zinfandel and Barbera can challenge and even surpass their counterparts from Italy—Chianti and the Barberas.

RECOMMENDED WINES

Red

Barbera	under $5
Cabernet Sauvignon	about $5
Pinot Noir	about $5
Cabernet Sauvignon Private Reserve	about $8

White

Pinot Chardonnay	about $5

SCHRAMSBERG

Calistoga, Napa County

The glorious uniqueness of the Schramsberg sparkling wines was well known even before February 1972, when twenty-five cases accompanied the presidential party to the People's Republic of China for the banquet attended by Mao Tse-tung. Since those toasts in Peking the tiny rationings sent to cities around the nation disappear even more quickly than before.

Jack Davies, Schramsberg's owner, has revived a historic old cellar, and he

Jack Davies turning champagne bottles at Schramsberg

produces what are unquestionably the best sparkling wines in the United States. Schramsberg's sparkling wines will remain dear and scarce for at least another decade. The lovely, light Blanc de Blancs is brut, or quite dry, in the French style. Made from a blend of Chardonnay and white Pinot grapes, it improves after several years in bottle. Schramsberg Cuvée de Gamay, made from the Napa Gamay and Pinot Noir grapes, is also dry, but delicately salmon-colored. For dessert champagne, the Crémant is unsurpassed.

RECOMMENDED WINES

Sparkling

Blanc de Blancs	about $9
Blanc de Noirs	about $11

SEBASTIANI

Sonoma County

August and Sam Sebastiani will not sell their vineyards and winery despite offers from corporations across the country.

The dedication and commitment all the Sebastianis feel to their homestead in Sonoma County are reflected in their big, honest, sturdy wines. Not the least of these is the robust, Italian-style Barbera, long the pride of the family and certainly one of the most pleasant varietal wines in all California. At the other end of the heartiness scale is a rather recent offering, a Beaujolais Nouveau that captures much of the light freshness which has made French wine of the same name so popular. The wine comes from the fine Gamay grape and is sometimes bottled within two months after the harvest, an ideal wine to be served slightly chilled.

RECOMMENDED WINES

Red

Gamay Beaujolais	about $3

Facing: Sebastiani Vineyards tasting room

North Coast Pinot Noir	under $5
Barbera	about $3
Cabernet Sauvignon	about $4

White

Sonoma Gewürztraminer	about $3

SIMI WINERY
Healdsburg, Sonoma County

At the famous Four Seasons restaurant in New York City, American wines are featured. At the top of the distinguished selection of fine California wines is a Simi Cabernet Sauvignon of 1935. Besides being rare, the wine is alive, well-balanced, and in its way reminiscent of old claret. It bears testimony to the greatness and long life of which California wines are capable. Enologist Mary Ann Graf and consultant André Tchelistcheff make a great deal of wine in a variety of styles. If you do not know which Simi to sample first, start by tasting their more recent Cabernet Sauvignon, Carignane, or Zinfandel. Some excellent whites have recently been harvested.

RECOMMENDED WINES

Red

Pinot Noir	under $5
Cabernet Sauvignon	about $3

White

Gewürztraminer	under $5
Pinot Chardonnay	about $5

Rosé

Cabernet Rosé	under $5

PARDUCCI
Ukiah, Mendocino County

At the close of World War I, Adolph Parducci began making wine in Sonoma County in the style of his Italian forebears.

Adolph's son John moved north to Ukiah in 1931.

There is a style to the Parducci wines. The reds are truly excellent. Some are unfiltered and unfined (an unfined wine has not had mineral or organic substances added to clarify and stabilize it), and you will find depth and sturdiness in their remarkable Cabernet Sauvignon and Zinfandel. As with great European wines, many of them will throw a deposit with the passage of time, thus evidencing vitality even after a decade in bottle.

But John Parducci was not content with the status quo. In 1972, after he had set the tone for all the big Mendocino reds, he became fascinated by the possibilities of long fermentation at low temperatures. This method, in California as well as in Europe, results in wines that are fresh, fruity, well-mannered (smooth and with no rough edges), and quick to mature. It is now the style of a great many vineyards in Bordeaux and Burgundy for making wine that requires less bottle aging before it is ready to drink.

If you find one of the "old" Parducci wines, you will enjoy a big, fat red in the tradition of Hermitage Rouge. If you run across the reds being produced now, you will be delighted with the fruity elegance. In either event, a good bottle.

RECOMMENDED WINES

Red

Gamay Beaujolais	under $5

White

Chenin Blanc	under $3

DAVID BRUCE
Los Gatos, Santa Clara County

David Bruce, a busy dermatologist practicing in San Jose and living close to the vineyards, developed a great interest in enology. In 1961 he built his home and winery at a 2,000-foot altitude in the hills above Los Gatos. Until recently Dr. Bruce sold his wines only by mail order. Now the repute of the vineyard is such that he is beginning to introduce his wines in various retail outlets. Convinced that his 1969 Chardonnay is as good as the best of the Montrachets, he charged the Montrachet price of $22 a bottle and sold out promptly. He has conducted such experiments as making a white wine from the Zinfandel grape and vinifying the Grenache grape as though he were making a white wine and not a red or a rosé.

RECOMMENDED WINES

Red
Petite Sirah   over $5
Zinfandel   over $8

White
Pinot Chardonnay   over $8

ALMADÉN VINEYARDS
Los Gatos, Santa Clara County
In 1967 the Almadén Vineyards became the property of National Distillers. Today Almadén is a giant, cultivating more than 8,000 acres of vineyard land in Santa Clara, Alameda, San Benito, and Monterey counties. Each year 6 million cases of wine are moved out their doors. Their range of wines is vast—over fifty Almadén labels are dispatched, including generics, varietals, champagnes, vermouths, sherries, and ports. It is a rare college student indeed who is not familiar with the large, graceful half-gallon and gallon bottles of Almadén Mountain Red and White.

RECOMMENDED WINES

Red
Monterey Zinfandel   about $3

White
Monterey Chenin Blanc   about $3

Rosé
Grenache Rosé   under $3

CHALONE
Soledad, Monterey County
This unique vineyard situated on the mountain crests 2,000 feet above the Salinas Valley makes great wines. Producing the wine by hand, winemaker Dick Graff uses traditional and painstaking techniques. Obviously, quantity is limited. Chalone whites are some of the most intense, powerful, and rich wines in the state.

RECOMMENDED WINES

Red
Pinot Noir   over $8

White
Chenin Blanc   about $5
Pinot Chardonnay   over $8

CONCANNON VINEYARDS
Livermore, Alameda County
This vineyard, founded in 1883 by James Concannon, an immigrant from Ireland and a religious man, was saved from the disaster of Prohibition because it had long been skilled in producing sacramental wines.

When the Archbishop of San Francisco needed altar wines, Concannon's wines filled that need. Although the old sacramental wines still constitute one-fourth of their production, Concannon is more famous now for their fine white table wines.

RECOMMENDED WINES

Red
Petite Sirah   under $5

White
Sauvignon Blanc   about $3
Johannisberg Riesling   under $5

53

PAUL MASSON VINEYARDS

Saratoga, Santa Clara County

The origins of the Paul Masson and Almadén vineyards are interlocked. In 1852, Etienne Thée, a winemaker from Bordeaux, planted his vineyard in Santa Clara County. His son-in-law, Charles Lefranc, succeeded him and was later joined by *his* son-in-law, Paul Masson, a Burgundian whose family had been *vignerons* for three hundred years. Eventually Masson started his own company, and later the original Lefranc-Masson winery and villa were bought by Almadén. Both Masson and Almadén can lay claim to being California's oldest commercial winegrowers, since both stem from Etienne Thée's original vineyard, where grapes have been grown continuously since 1852.

With financial support from Seagram, Paul Masson has become a wine giant and now produces and sells annually over 3 million cases of California wine, some of it going to Europe and Asia. The source of most of the varietal table wine is their vast 7,000-acre Pinnacles Vineyard in Monterey. They do not vintage their wine but prefer blending two or more vintage years to achieve roundness, balance, and readiness for consumption soon after bottling.

RECOMMENDED WINES

Red
Cabernet Sauvignon Pinnacles   about $5

White
Emerald Dry   about $3
Chenin Blanc   about $3

Sparkling
Brut   about $5

MIRASSOU VINEYARDS

San Jose, Santa Clara County

In the mid-nineteenth century, two French immigrants founded neighboring vineyards in the Santa Clara Valley within the space of seven years. One was Pierre Mirassou, who started his winery in 1854. The other was Pierre Pellier, who in 1861 planted his vineyard with vines brought from France. Shortly after Pellier had established the winery, his daughter married Pierre Mirassou, and the Mirassou branch of the family eventually assumed control of all the winemaking operations.

A few years ago, pressured by crowded Santa Clara, the Mirassous, along with Paul Masson, planted vineyards in Monterey County. There, using the latest technology, combined with their five generations of experience, they are making exceptional wines.

Typical Mirassou wines are clean, fresh, and fruity, with a distinctive California personality.

RECOMMENDED WINES

Red
Pinot Noir   about $5

White
Burgundy   about $3
Chenin Blanc   about $3

Sparkling
Au Naturel   about $8

THE NOVITIATE OF LOS GATOS

Los Gatos, Santa Clara County

As with the Christian Brothers, making wine and supporting a number of schools go hand in hand for the brothers in Los Gatos. The Novitiate has been making altar wines since 1888. Only about one-third of their production reaches the general public, but they have plans for expansion. Ultimately, distribution should reach all the large cities in the United States. All their wines are sound, pleasant, and moderately priced. None bears a vintage, but all are fully matured when offered for sale.

RECOMMENDED WINE

White

Muscat de Frontignan   about $5

RIDGE VINEYARDS

Cupertino, Santa Clara County

Three miles of slow, treacherous driving along Montebello Road will bring you to an altitude of 2,600 feet and the Ridge vineyard. The 45-acre vineyard is predominantly planted with Zinfandel, supplemented by Cabernet Sauvignon, Chardonnay, and Merlot. Ridge has set out to prove that Zinfandel can be as bold, deep-colored, complex, and long-lived as the best of California Cabernet Sauvignons. Tasting their Zinfandel is an astonishing experience. The wine is almost unbelievable, full of sheer intensity and power. All the wines produced here are vintage-labeled and unfiltered. Some connoisseurs claim that elegance is sacrificed for the sake of bigness, but no one interested in experiencing the drama of good California wine should fail to acquire at least one bottle of Ridge's Zinfandel.

RECOMMENDED WINES

Red

Zinfandel   about $8
Cabernet Sauvignon   over $8

White

Pinot Chardonnay   about $8

SAN MARTIN VINEYARDS

San Martin, Santa Clara County

San Martin, a large old winery long run by the Felice family, was acquired by a Texas company in 1972. Good medium-priced wines are available from San Martin, but watch for this to change in the future. San Martin has been purchased by Somerset Wine Company, a division of Norton Simon, Inc., headed by Alexis Lichine and Terence Clancy. Given Lichine's knowledge and expertise, we can expect innovative development and new directions for this winery. By 1980, San Martin will undoubtedly be a name to reckon with in California wine.

RECOMMENDED WINE

Red

Zinfandel   under $5

WENTE BROS.

Livermore, Alameda County

The winery of Wente Bros. is the second-oldest family-owned vineyard in the Livermore Valley. White wines are the most popular product of the valley, and have been the specialty of Wente Bros. since Carl H. Wente, grandfather of the present head of the company, came from Germany nearly a century ago. Wente white wines have an impressive pedigree: many of their vine cuttings came, at the turn of the century, from the Count de Lur-Saluces's famous Château d'Yquem vineyard of Bordeaux.

The Wentes were among the first in California to produce top-quality Pinot Chardonnay in any quantity. One of the fine California selections Frank Schoonmaker brought to national attention about thirty years ago was Wente Chardonnay. Another was their Sauvignon Blanc, still a smooth, elegant wine with a slightly sweet edge betraying its Sauternes heritage. Pinot Blanc, a Burgundy wine grape that most experts think less good than the noble Pinot Chardonnay, has never been a true star in the galaxy of California wines, but the talent of the Wentes and the soil of the Livermore Valley join to make an excellent vintage Pinot Blanc.

The Wentes' flair for white wines is not limited to varietals. Astute, artistic blenders, they have combined Chenin Blanc

55

from the Loire with Ugni Blanc from Cognac, creating a charming wine called Blanc de Blancs.

RECOMMENDED WINES

White

Blanc de Blancs	about $3
Johannisberg Riesling	about $3
Pinot Chardonnay	under $5
Johannisberg Riesling Spätlese	about $5

WEIBEL CHAMPAGNE VINEYARDS
Mission San Jose, Santa Clara County

The Weibel winery stands on the site of the old Warm Springs Hotel. In 1869 Leland Stanford, California Governor and Senator, as well as railroad magnate, bought the large tract of land where the hotel had stood and planted about 100 acres of vines. Later he gave the vineyard to his brother Josiah. Phylloxera destroyed the vineyard at the end of the century, and it lay dormant until 1945, when Rudolph Weibel, a recent arrival from Switzerland, bought the land and planted vines, naming his establishment the Weibel Champagne Vineyards. The Chardonnay Brut Champagne bearing the Weibel label is bottle-fermented, fresh, well-balanced, and truly excellent. You will discover Weibel's champagne bearing many different labels because his vineyards also make private-label champagnes for many hotels and stores across the country. Most of the Weibel table wines are made at the handsome new winery in Mendocino.

RECOMMENDED WINE

Sparkling

Brut	about $5

THE MONTEREY VINEYARD
Gonzales, Monterey County

This group has undertaken one of the most daring and important wine ventures in California history. They have acquired 10,000 acres, probably the largest single vineyard in the world, and are planting it with superior varietals.

The first vintage from this exciting new vineyard was the 1974 harvest of Chenin Blanc and Grüner Sylvaner, Gamay Beaujolais, Chardonnay, and Johannisberg Riesling. The dedication is there but the unknown factors are the soil and the climate. We must wait until 1980 before judging this new vineyard.

RECOMMENDED WINES

Red

Gamay Beaujolais	about $3
Zinfandel	about $3

White

Del Mar Ranch	under $3
Chenin Blanc	about $3

CALLAWAY VINEYARD & WINERY
Temecula, Riverside County

Ely Callaway, retired president of Burlington Industries, gave up the world of big business for a modest vineyard not far from Newport Beach. There, his vines thrive atop a coastal ridge where the normally scorching heat of southern California is tempered by cool Pacific breezes. The small, handsomely equipped winery draws on the best wine technology of northern California neighbors, and of France and Germany as well. In fact, Callaway's winemaker is formerly of Schloss Vollrads in the Rheingau. We've been enthusiastic about Callaway wines since first tasting them, and are convinced that their excellence may well lure more premium wineries to the southern part of the state.

RECOMMENDED WINES

Red

Zinfandel	about $5

White

Chenin Blanc	under $5
White Riesling	about $5

GALLO VINEYARDS (E. & J. GALLO)
Modesto, San Joaquin Valley

Thanks to popular wines and substantial advertising, California's biggest winery is also its most famous. Because of the quality control maintained by a large and creative staff of enologists and technicians, Gallo wines are noticeably better than the typical French, Italian, or Spanish ordinary table wines. All the wines are slightly sweet, since Gallo stops their fermentation at the moment when a small amount of unconverted sugar remains in the musts. Most Americans like their wines with a slight trace of sweetness, but as tastes change, Gallo wine will certainly become drier.

RECOMMENDED WINES

Red

Hearty Burgundy Red	magnums about $3

White

Chablis Blanc	magnums about $3

FRANZIA BROTHERS WINERY
Ripon, San Joaquin Valley

Now the property of the Coca-Cola Bottling Company of New York, Franzia, like Gallo, buys grapes from all over the state. Expensive, select varieties are purchased from large vineyards in Napa and Sonoma to add character and complexity to the wines.

RECOMMENDED WINES

Red

Zinfandel	half-gallons under $3

Rosé

Vin Rosé	half-gallons under $3

GUILD WINE COMPANY
Lodi, San Joaquin Valley

The third-largest winery in the state, Guild produces its wines at five different locations from grapes supplied by a cooperative of some five hundred members. Guild has three major brands: Famiglia Cribari, the sweetest line; Vino da Tavola, the familiar label with the red-checked tablecloth design; and Winemasters, perhaps the best.

RECOMMENDED WINES

Red

Vino da Tavola

Red	half-gallons under $3
Winemasters Zinfandel	
	half-gallons about $4

White

Vino da Tavola

White	half-gallons under $3

FICKLIN VINEYARDS
Madera, San Joaquin Valley

In complete contrast to the giant wineries producing millions of gallons of table wines for everyday consumption is a small vineyard that makes a few cases of the best dessert wine produced in the United States. Walter Ficklin makes port wines, and without a doubt they are some of the best examples of the type grown outside Portugal. Only the grapes that give the original Portuguese wine go into Ficklin port—Tinta Cão, Tinta Madera, and Touriga. The wine is so popular with a small circle of California wine enthusiasts that, unfortunately, little finds its way outside the state.

RECOMMENDED WINES

Tinta Cão Port	about $5
Tinta Madera Port	about $5

THE VINEYARDS OF NEW YORK STATE

New York State, though second only to California in total wine production, has a much smaller output. California has some 600,000 acres of vineyards, yielding about 300 million gallons of wine annually; the 40,000 acres of vines in New York State produce only about 15 million gallons each harvest.

Nature is kinder in California; the hours of bright sunshine are long, and the growing season is seldom shortened by a killing frost in autumn. There the *Vitis vinifera,* with its sensitivity to cold, can reach maturity in almost carefree fashion. This gentle weather is not found in New York State, and it is only recently that any vines save the hardy *Vitis labrusca* native to the East could survive the sub-zero temperatures of January and February. The Catawbas, Concords, and Delawares had their vogue, but today most experts think we pay a price in flavor for American wines made from American grapes. Catawba and the other labruscas give a heavy taste, an overpowering aroma, and only simple character to their wines—the composite effect called "foxy."

Winemakers in the Eastern states have tried to make their wines more like classic European ones. They now have a new friend—a large family of vines known as the French-American hybrids. The new strains may not give us all the breed, depth, and finesse found in wines made of vinifera grapes, but they combine some of the best vinifera traits with a constitution hearty enough for the rigors of a New York State winter.

More recent than the hybrid revolution is a trend that may eventually help Eastern winemakers produce more and even better wines in the European style. Dr. Konstantin Frank, a true pioneer, has jumped the hybrid hurdle and has managed to grow the delicate *Vitis vinifera* vines themselves in New York State.

At some of the larger producers it is particularly interesting to note the tremendous quantities of champagne and other sparkling wines; half of the total United States consumption is supplied by New York State. Fortified wines also play a big part at the wineries. These fortified wines are usually blended with neutral wines and brandy from California. Few spirits stores in America do not carry a New York State sherry or port.

Following are brief descriptions of the leading wineries of New York State, with recommendations of some of their best wines. These selected bottles are generally available throughout the East but may not be so easily found in other parts of the country. Price levels are those prevailing in New York City. Suggestions about vintage years appear on page 157.

Gathering grapes in the vineyard at Marlboro-on-the-Hudson, c. 1890

BENMARL VINEYARDS

Marlboro, Hudson Valley

Benmarl has helped to speed the revival of this important winegrowing region. Many vines grew along the river north of New York City in the last century. Yet only in the past two decades have vintners come again to cultivate the land and make wine.

Mark Miller and his family are the heart of Benmarl. While working as an illustrator in the Burgundy region of France, Miller came to know and love good wine. Benmarl means "slate hill" in Gaelic, an apt description of the earth Miller chose for his vines. He grows French-American hybrids and a little Chardonnay. Here, as at the other New York State vineyards planted in hybrid vines, white wines seem to do better than reds.

RECOMMENDED WINES

Red

Baco Noir   under $5

White

Seyval Blanc   under $5

BOORDY VINEYARD

Penn Yan, Finger Lakes

In 1968 the president of a big grape juice and applesauce concern approached Philip Wagner with the idea of making his popular Boordy wines in New York and Washington State instead of only at Wagner's little homestead in Maryland. Soon two giant plants of the Seneca Foods Corporation were making wine under Wagner's supervision. Now each of the Boordy bottles states its origin—Maryland, New York, or Washington. It is Wagner's goal for each of the far-flung Boordy wineries to make a distinctive regional wine, to be known, as wines are in Europe, by the name of the area where the grapes were grown and vinified.

Boordy Vineyard's harvest at the original Maryland winery

All the Boordy wines are light and simple, ideal everyday table wines. The original red, white, and rosé and some of the other blends are made from the French-American hybrids that Wagner insists are the hope for high-quality, inexpensive Eastern wine. Vinifera vines, too, now grow in the Boordy New York vineyards.

RECOMMENDED WINES

Red

Cabernet Sauvignon   about $3

White

Semillon Sec   under $3

Chenin Blanc   about $3

TAYLOR WINE COMPANY

Hammondsport, Finger Lakes

Despite its humble origin as a 7-acre vineyard, the company is now a large, successful public corporation that annually sells over 3 million cases of wine. Taylor acquired the famed Great Western brand and winery in 1961, making the new combine one of the largest wine producers in the East.

Walter Taylor, owner of Bully Hill Vineyards

Their well-advertised brands of sparkling wines sell in vast quantities throughout the United States. The best of the Taylor champagnes is the Brut, with a good medium-dry flavor and the foxy taste of the Eastern grape that differentiates it from French champagne. Taylor also produces Cold Duck, that blend of sparkling Burgundy and champagne which took Americans by storm but is waning in popularity.

At this winery, table wines are not ignored. Much of what is blended into their wines, particularly the fortified ones, is shipped from wineries in California. Taylor Wine Company was bought by Coca-Cola in 1976.

RECOMMENDED WINE

White
Emerald Riesling   under $3

GOLD SEAL VINEYARDS
Hammondsport, Finger Lakes
During the early 1960s two extraordinary winemakers met at the Gold Seal Vineyards. One came from France, Charles Fournier, formerly the manager of Veuve Clicquot Champagne. The other, Dr. Konstantin Frank, came from Germany and Russia (he had been educated in Odessa). It was a happy meeting, because these two zealous gentlemen experimentally planted Chardonnay, Johannisberg Riesling, and French-American hybrids. Eventually Dr. Frank left to establish his own vineyard.

While the management shows no sign of abandoning the dependable and profitable pursuit of making champagne and rather sweet wines from a variety of native labrusca grapes, they are moving more and more in the direction of the superior

61

French-American hybrids as well as Chardonnay and Pinot Noir.

There are 500 acres under cultivation, but they supply only a small percentage of the grapes required by this giant winery. The balance comes from almost two hundred independent growers in the area.

RECOMMENDED WINES

White

Chablis Nature	under $3
Pinot Chardonnay	about $3

Sparkling

Brut	about $5

At Great Western, staves are used to separate the champagne bottles

BULLY HILL VINEYARDS
Hammondsport, Finger Lakes

At these vineyards, once owned by his grandfather, who founded the Taylor Wine Company in 1880, Walter Taylor devotes himself to making natural wines. Even though it is legal in New York State under certain circumstances to add up to 35 percent water and sugar, he shuns the addition of ingredients often used to raise the alcohol level and balance the wine. "Wine without water" is his slogan.

Taylor concentrates on the best of the French-American hybrids. His bottles proudly bear both the vintage date and the varietal name. "A wine label is like a person's face," says Taylor. "It should tell you what you want to know about him."

RECOMMENDED WINES

Red

Chelois Noir	about $3

White

Aurora Blanc	about $3

GREAT WESTERN
Hammondsport, Finger Lakes

Great Western was merged with the Taylor Wine Company in 1961. Its claim to fame is a champagne that has won awards in European competitions and has been a consistent favorite at wedding parties in this country.

The company is the oldest in the area, proudly displaying over the front porch an antique sign that reads, "New York Bonded Winery No. 1."

RECOMMENDED WINES

Red

Baco Noir	under $3

White

Duchess	under $3

Sparkling

Brut	about $5
Natural	about $5

VINIFERA VINEYARDS
Hammondsport, Finger Lakes

Dr. Konstantin Frank owns scarcely 60 acres of vineyards. Few wineshops sell his wines. Yet Dr. Frank's contribution to winemaking in eastern America is at once simple and overwhelming: he has grown

The Hammondsport depot serves the single-track railroad nicknamed "The Champagne Trail"

and made wonderful wines from *Vitis vinifera* grapes. His Rieslings, Gewürztraminers, and Pinot Chardonnay vines are the first links joining the relatively backward vineyards of the eastern United States with the mainstream of viticulture around the world. His wines are good, and worthy of their place in American wine history.

RECOMMENDED WINES

Red
Cabernet Sauvignon   about $5

White
Gewürztraminer   under $5
Pinot Chardonnay   under $5
Johannisberg Riesling   about $5

WIDMER'S WINE CELLARS
Naples, Finger Lakes
Sherries make up only a small part of the Widmer production. Here one can discover the familiar listings of labrusca-flavored generics and fortified dessert wines. The best wines bear the simple, honest American names—such varietals as Lake Niagara, Delaware, and Elvira.

Like many of its New York State brethren, Widmer is firmly allied with the native labrusca and the French-American hybrids. Unlike its neighbors, this ambitious winery has made the cross-country leap and expanded into one of the best winegrowing regions of California, the Alexander Valley of Sonoma County. There they have planted a sizable vineyard with European grape varieties. Departing from their past practices, they will be bottling Cabernet Sauvignon, Pinot Noir, and Chardonnay.

RECOMMENDED WINES

White
Delaware   under $3
Foch   under $3

HOW TO READ A NEW YORK STATE WINE LABEL

Since many of the grapes grown in New York are the strongly flavored *Vitis labrusca*, the resultant overpoweringly foxy taste is often neutralized by the addition of bland wines from California or elsewhere. By state law, no more than 25 percent of the grapes used to make a particular wine may come from another state or country. No more than 35 percent of the total sugar content may be artificially supplied by the vintner.

Vintage date
At least 95 percent of the grape named on the bottle was grown, harvested, and fermented in the year stated.

The appellation "New York State"
At least 75 percent of the wine in the bottle was produced from grapes grown in New York State.

The appellation "American"
The vintner crushed, fermented, matured, and bottled at least 75 percent of the wine in the bottle.

Estate-bottled
All the grapes that went into the wine were grown by the vintner; he made all the wine and bottled it himself.

Varietal name
As in California, at least 51 percent of the wine must come from the grape named on the label.

"LAKE COUNTRY" WINE

"Lake Country Red" is a vague expression that has no legal definition. Under state law, 25 percent of wines from outside the state, plus a limited dosage of sugar and water, can be added.

ESTATE-BOTTLING IN THE EAST

The back label tells all—facts of the vintage, the grapes that went into the wine, and that it was estate-bottled. Note that the grape varieties are all French-American hybrids.

A KOSHER SACRAMENTAL WINE

Despite the religious cast of the label, most of this wine is consumed as a table wine by the general public. Since "New York State" does not appear on the label, the wine can come from anywhere, literally.

AMERICA'S BEST-SELLING CHAMPAGNE

"Brut" means that this is the driest champagne made by Great Western. The wine was fermented in the bottle by the classic French method. Note the founding date and the awards it has won.

OTHER RECOMMENDED WINES OF NORTH AMERICA

OHIO

Red

Meier's Château Jac-Jan
  Ohio Valley Red   about $3

White

Tarula Farm's White   under $3
Isle St. George Dessert Wine   about $3

MICHIGAN

Red

Tabor Hill Baco Noir   about $3

VERMONT

Vermont Vineyards Apple Wine   under $3

MASSACHUSETTS

White

Chicama Vineyards Chardonnay   about $5

WASHINGTON

White

Ste. Michelle Chenin Blanc   about $4

CANADA

Red

Château Gai Burgundy   about $3

White

Bright's Pinot Chardonnay   about $4

MEXICO

Red

Santo Tomás Cabernet Sauvignon about $3

TABOR HILL
VINEYARD

**1973
BACO NOIR**

GROWN AND BOTTLED BY TABOR HILL VINEYARD AND
WINECELLAR, INC., BERRIEN COUNTY, MICHIGAN
ALCOHOL 12% BY VOLUME

The first new Michigan winery in 25 years,
Tabor Hill makes vintage, estate-bottled wines

Santo Tomás varietal wines reflect modern
improvements made in Mexico's oldest winery

THE
WINES
OF
FRANCE

France produces the largest number of the world's finest wines: Chambertin, Château Lafite, La Tâche, Château Margaux, Le Montrachet, Château d'Yquem are but a few illustrious names on a list that could easily be multiplied twenty times over. The roll of near-greats could be even longer: whole regions, such as Chablis and Champagne, produce wines of such matchless character that their would-be imitators elsewhere in the world might be wise to call their wines—pleasant as they may be—by other names.

These classic wines of France exist for reasons both obvious and obscure. Why should the grapevine give great wine when it grows in soil that is often too poor for any other crop? Vines seem to prefer soil pebbled with gravel and chalky with calcium, containing scant but balanced traces of several important minerals. Each layer of subsoil through which the deep roots of the vine penetrate offers its own elements to the grape, ultimately to contribute bouquet and taste to the finished wine. Not only the makeup of vineyard soil but the precise situation of the ground is critical—its particular tilt to the warm, nourishing rays of the sun. And beyond these elements there are others we still do not understand. Why should Chambertin have so much more depth and balance than a wine grown only a hundred yards away in the very same commune? Why is Château Petrus superior to any other Pomerol?

No matter how perfect the exposure of a vineyard, the number of hours of sunshine it will enjoy during the growing season is also a question of weather. Yet the best vineyards of France seem to make consistently fine wines even in years when the weather has been unfavorable and the district as a whole has done poorly.

This brings us to another crucial factor, the winemaker himself. Great wine is no accident, for, given the best of natural conditions, the man who makes it must be perfectly attuned to the needs of his vines and wines. It is he who must determine the moment to begin the harvest so as to pick the grapes at their peak. Once the crop is in, he has to keep careful watch over the process of fermentation. Each step requires his minute attention, and every great winemaker has certain secrets that help to maintain his wine's high reputation.

Another reason for the premier position of French wines is the strict controls established by the growers themselves and enforced by the French government. The laws of *Appellation Contrôlée* guarantee the wine drinker that a given wine is the genuine article, meeting the standards that have been set for it.

A carved panel with the motto *In Vino Veritas* is from Château Ducru-Beaucaillou, which makes a Second Growth St.-Julien

Facing: From a banquet to a picnic, there is a French wine for all occasions. A pleasant Côte de Provence red, cooled in icy water, is delightful with an outdoor lunch.
© Arnold Newman

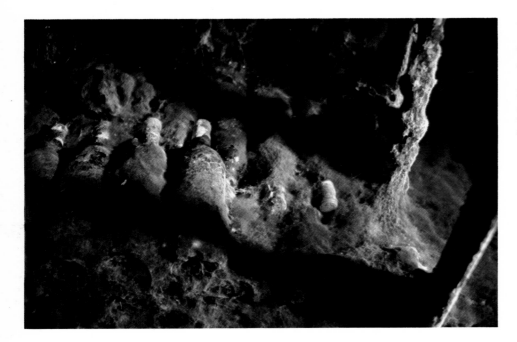

At Château Lafite-Rothschild the "library" of old bottles contains cobweb-encrusted relics of great vintages going back to 1797

Burgundian wines and food at a banquet of the Confrérie des Chevaliers du Tastevin in the Château de Vougeot
© Arnold Newman

A regional wine such as Bordeaux Rouge carries the simplest and broadest designation for the vast assortment of red Bordeaux wines. But within the region there are districts such as Médoc, Pomerol, and Graves whose wines are subject to higher and more specific standards than the simpler regional wines. Within the district are the communes (parishes), whose standards are higher still. Like the concentric circles on a target, the place of origin contracts and grows smaller as it becomes more specific: the whole is the region of Bordeaux, the outer circles are the districts, the inner ones are the communes. The great vineyards represent the bull's-eye. In Burgundy this system reaches even greater refinement, since each *Grand Cru* (Great Growth) vineyard has its own legal *Appellation* and is not required to show a commune name.

Although vineyards with *Appellation Contrôlée* status are to be found in virtually all the major wine districts of France, only 10 to 15 percent of the nearly 2 billion gallons of French wine produced annually qualify for the designation. The rest is largely the *vin ordinaire* the Frenchman drinks daily or the *vins du pays*, the local country wines that travelers in France often find so agreeable. Happily, most of what is imported into the United States is *Appellation Contrôlée*, the best that France has to offer. Some wines of the rank below *Appellation Contrôlée* also reach us. These are the wines with a label bearing the letters V.D.Q.S. (*Vin Délimité de Qualité Supérieure*) that make for pleasant casual drinking.

In the pages that follow, you will find our favorite French wines listed after each section. All prices for recommended wines are for recent vintages, within the past ten years. Prices will vary, depending upon the quality of a specific year. Consult the vintage chart on page 149 for which years to seek out and which to avoid, but don't follow the chart rigidly. With some pleasant effort you may discover low-priced, good-tasting wines from vintages with lower ratings.

ESCRITEAU

PREMIÈRE ASSIETTE
Les Grands Pourcheux en leur Gelée & le Jambon Persillé Dijonnaise
relevés de bonne Moutarde Forte de Dijon
escortés d'un Bourgogne Aligoté 1966 frais et gouleyant
de Pernand-Vergelesses

DEUXIÈME ASSIETTE
Les Soufflés de Brochet Truffés Nantua
humidifiés d'un Meursault Genevrières 1966 suédé et bouqueté
Domaine Prosper

ENTREMETS
La Fricassée de Coquelets aux Morilles
accompagnée d'un Côte de Nuits Villages 1964 soyeux et prenant

RÔTI
Les Jambon Rôtis Printaniers
arrosés d'un Chambolle-Musigny 1962 suave et caressant

ISSUE DE TABLE
Le Véritable Cîteaux et ses Compagnons Fromagers d'Ailleurs
rehaussé d'un Vosne-Romanée 1962 de mémorable lignée
Malconsorts

BOUTEHORS
Le Pousse au Clos de Vougeot en Nervosmes
l'Ananas en Glace — Les Mignardises Bourgignottes
Les Passiots de Fruits

Le Café Noir de Chicole le Vieux Marc, la Prunelle de Bourgogne
par solenne, et réconfortante

BORDEAUX

esides being one of the finest wine regions of France, Bordeaux is the largest, with 200,000 acres planted in vines, more than twice as many as Burgundy. Half the wine of Bordeaux is red, half white. The division is roughly geographical, since the reds come mainly from the northern areas and the whites from the south. An exception is the district of Graves, which makes both red and white, with white predominating. The British have long called the red Bordeaux wines "claret" (a corruption of the old French *clairet*, the name of a pale red wine first shipped to England in the twelfth century). Today the word may refer to any light-bodied red wine (it is commonly so used by vintners in Spain and California). In wine-drinking circles the name "claret" is synonymous with good red Bordeaux.

The primary grape varieties used for making red wine in Bordeaux are Cabernet Sauvignon and Merlot, with supporting roles played by Malbec, Cabernet Franc, and Petit-Verdot. In some of the vineyard districts, one of the latter three may dominate the plantings. For white wines the Sémillon and Sauvignon Blanc are most important, with Merlot Blanc and Muscadelle used to a small extent. In order to give their wines balance and harmony or to counter the overpowering influence of any single grape, most vineyards are planted in more than one variety.

Proud of its products and eager to maintain its high standards, the wine trade of Bordeaux has rated the local wines in order of quality. Attempts to rank the many different wines go back several centuries, but perhaps the most complete is the famous 1855 classification of Médoc wines (see page 83). Most of the other leading districts of Bordeaux also have fixed ratings, though none is so complex or comprehensive as that of the Médoc.

That a particular wine is included in a classification is one indication of its quality.

A candle held beneath the bottle while the wine is being poured shows up any sediment before it can reach the glass

Facing: Members of the Jurade de Saint-Émilion gather to celebrate the glories of their wines. Glasses are held by the stem or foot so they will not be smudged or warmed

Another warranty of excellence on the label of a fine wine is the phrase *Mis en bouteille au château*, or "Bottled at the château." This is the assurance by the grower that the wine in the bottle was made and bottled by him, that it was not blended or tampered with by anyone else. The names of the great châteaus are important, but so are those of the major Bordeaux shipping firms: Cordier, Cruse et Fils, Calvet, Barton et Guestier, William Bolter, Dourthe, Deluze, Eschenauer, Nathaniel Johnston, Kressmann, Alexis Lichine & Co., Schroder & Schÿler, Delor, Sichel et Fils.

RECOMMENDED REGIONAL BORDEAUX WINES

Red	*White*
All about $4	All about $4
Ch. Mouton-Cadet	Ch. Mouton-Cadet
Pontet-Latour	Pontet-Latour
B&G Prince Noir	Lichine Graves
Ginestet Haut-Médoc	
La Cour Pavillon	
Sichel My Cousin's Claret	
Lichine Médoc	

THE MÉDOC AND THE HAUT-MÉDOC

The incomparable red wines of the Médoc, and particularly of the Haut (Upper) Médoc, include some of the most famous in the world. For elegance, breed, and finesse (that is to say, fine-ness), they are unsurpassed. The tenacity of their staying power is often astonishing; it is not unusual to find the great wines from this district still good after sixty or seventy years. The celebrated communes of Margaux, Saint-Julien, Pauillac, and Saint-Estèphe are situated in the Haut-Médoc on the west bank of the Gironde. Margaux is near the southern end of the district, Saint-Estèphe is toward the north.

The best vineyards of these communes make up the First Growths of the 1855 classification, which also included Château Haut-Brion in neighboring Graves. When the classification was devised, the ranking was based on the prices the wines had brought over the previous century, prices that reflected the current value of the land and, presumably, the quality of the various wines. Most experts would make only a dozen or so changes in the standing of the sixty or so vineyards represented. Perhaps more amendments would be made to upgrade deserving vineyards (Mouton-Rothschild is a case in point) than to demote those making less interesting wines.

In the 1855 classification we are dealing with the nobility, the very best of the 6,000 vineyards of the Médoc; even the vineyard of the lowest rank can be considered a duke or an earl. To say that a Fourth Growth is only one-quarter as good as a First Growth is to miss the point. The variations in these sixty-odd wines of the 1855 classification are only a matter of degree, and very gradual degrees at that. In the array of wines in any good wineshop, châteaus officially ranked as Third or Fourth or Fifth Growths often claim prices as high as some Second Growths, and rightly so. Growers and shippers commonly refer to all the wines below the first category as Second Growths. First Growth prices reflect status as much as the intrinsic quality of the wine.

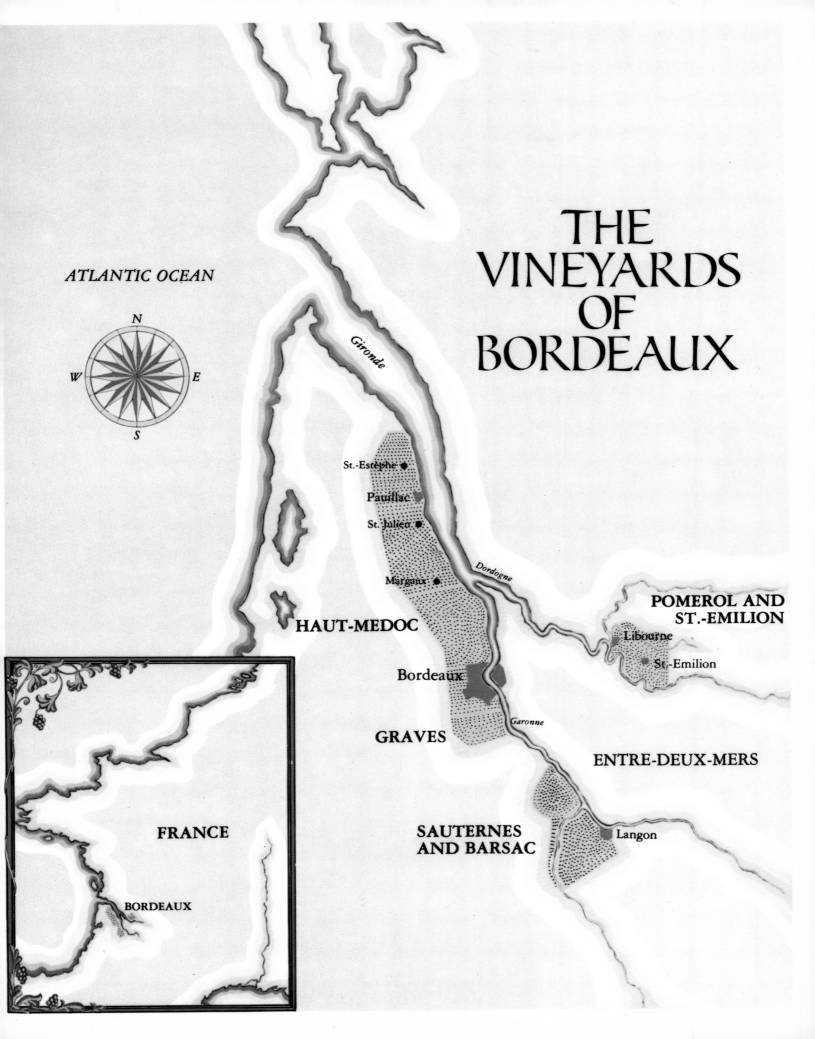

ATLANTIC OCEAN

N
W *E*
S

Gironde

THE
VINEYARDS
OF
BORDEAUX

St.-Estèphe ●

Pauillac ●

St.-Julien ●

Dordogne

Margaux ●

HAUT-MEDOC

POMEROL AND
ST.-EMILION

Libourne ●
● St.-Emilion

Bordeaux ●

GRAVES

Garonne

ENTRE-DEUX-MERS

SAUTERNES
AND BARSAC

Langon ●

FRANCE

BORDEAUX

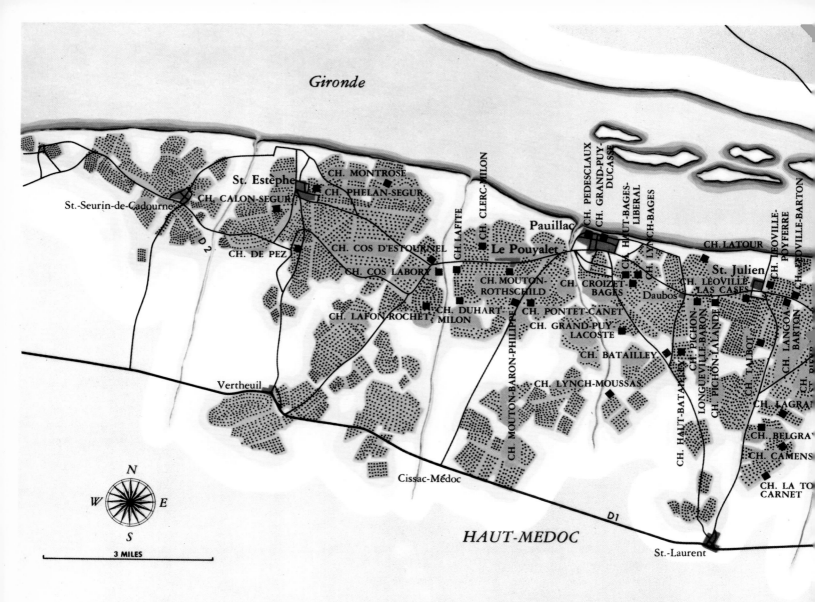

Gironde

St.-Seurin-de-Cadourne

St. Estèphe
CH. CALON-SEGUR
CH. MONTROSE
CH. PHELAN-SEGUR
CH. DE PEZ
CH. COS D'ESTOURNEL
CH. COS LABORY
CH. LAFON-ROCHET
CH. DUHART-MILON
CH. LAFITE
CH. CLERC-MILON

Vertheuil

Cissac-Médoc

CH. PEDESCLAUX
CH. GRAND-PUY-DUCASSE
CH. HAUT-BAGES-LIBERAL
CH. LYNCH-BAGES
Pauillac
Le Pouyalet
CH. MOUTON-ROTHSCHILD
CH. CROIZET-BAGES
CH. PONTET-CANET
CH. GRAND-PUY-LACOSTE
CH. MOUTON-BARON-PHILIPPE
CH. BATAILLEY
CH. LYNCH-MOUSSAS
Daubos

CH. LATOUR
St. Julien
CH. LÉOVILLE-LAS CASES
CH. LÉOVILLE-POYFERRE
CH. LÉOVILLE-BARTON
CH. PICHON-LONGUEVILLE-BARON
CH. PICHON-LALANDE
CH. HAUT-BATAILLEY
CH. TALBOT
CH. LANGOA-BARTON
CH. LAGRA
CH. BELGRA
CH. CAMENS
CH. LA TO CARNET

D 2

N
W E
S

3 MILES

HAUT-MEDOC
D 1
St.-Laurent

THE
HAUT-MEDOC
AND
GRAVES

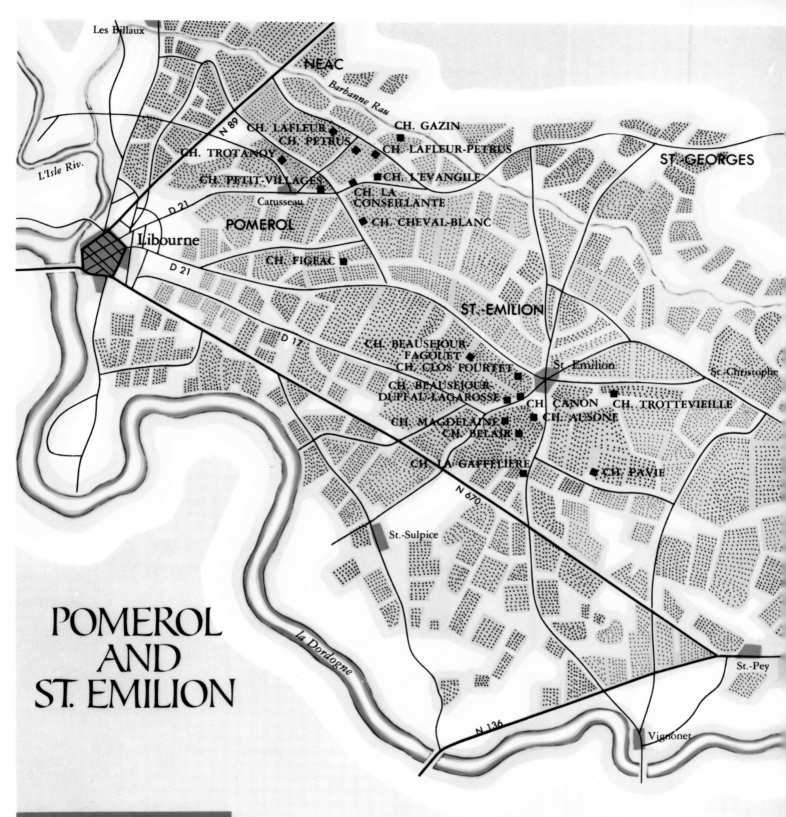

POMEROL
AND
ST. EMILION

Les Billaux

NEAC

Barbanne Rau

N 89

CH. LAFLEUR

CH. GAZIN

CH. PETRUS

CH. LAFLEUR-PETRUS

ST. GEORGES

CH. TROTANOY

CH. PETIT-VILLAGES

CH. L'EVANGILE

L'Isle Riv.

D 21

Catusseau

CH. LA CONSEILLANTE

POMEROL

CH. CHEVAL-BLANC

Libourne

D 21

CH. FIGEAC

ST.-EMILION

D 17

St. Christophe

CH. BEAUSEJOUR-FAGOUET

CH. CLOS FOURTET

St. Emilion

CH. BEAUSEJOUR-DUFFAU-LAGAROSSE

CH. CANON

CH. TROTTEVIEILLE

CH. MAGDELAINE

CH. AUSONE

CH. BELAIR

CH. LA GAFFELIERE

CH. PAVIE

N 670

St.-Sulpice

la Dordogne

St.-Pey

N 136

Vignonet

CHÂTEAU ROUGET

GRAND CRU
POMEROL
APPELLATION POMEROL CONTRÔLÉE

1967

Marcel BERTRAND, propriétaire à Pomerol (Gironde)

MIS EN BOUTEILLES AU CHÂTEAU

Clos-Fourtet

PREMIER GRAND CRU CLASSÉ

Saint-Emilion

APPELLATION SAINT-ÉMILION CONTRÔLÉE

François LURTON
PROPRIÉTAIRE
SAINT-ÉMILION

1969

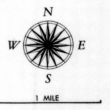

N
W E
S

1 MILE

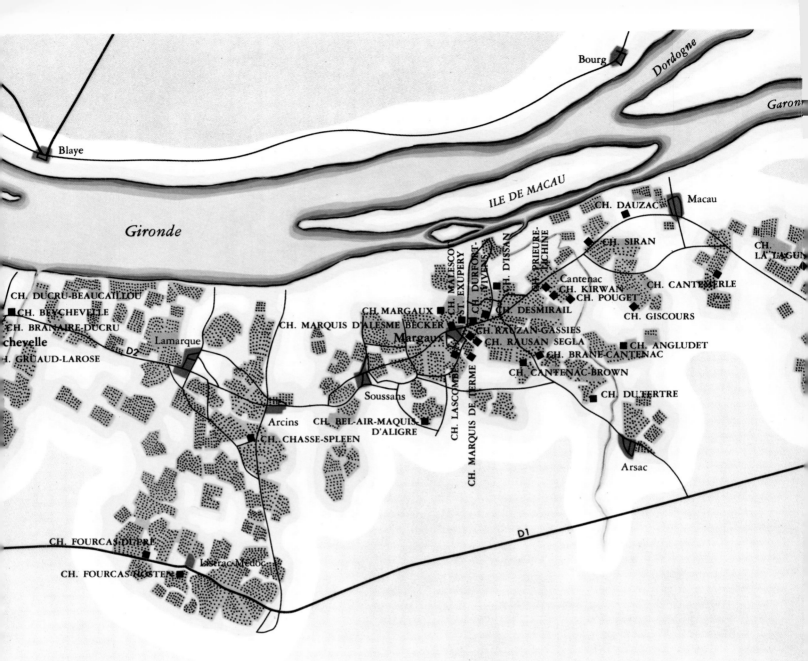

Bourg

Dordogne

Garonne

Blaye

Gironde

ILE DE MACAU

CH. DAUZAC

Macau

CH. SIRAN

CH. LA LAGUNE

CH. D'ISSAN

CH. PRIEURE-LICHINE

CH. DUCRU-BEAUCAILLOU

CH. BEYCHEVELLE

CH. BRANAIRE-DUCRU

Cantenac

CH. CANTEMERLE

chevelle

Lamarque

CH. MARQUIS D'ALESME BECKER

CH. MALESCO-ST. EXUPERY

CH. DURFORT-VIVENS

CH. KIRWAN

CH. POUGET

H. GRUAUD-LAROSE

D2

CH. MARGAUX

Margaux

CH. DESMIRAIL

CH. GISCOURS

CH. RAUZAN-GASSIES

CH. RAUSAN SEGLA

CH. ANGLUDET

CH. BRANE-CANTENAC

CH. CANTENAC-BROWN

Soussans

CH. LASCOMBE

CH. MARQUIS DE TERME

CH. DU TERTRE

Arcins

CH. BEL-AIR-MAQUIS-D'ALIGRE

CH. CHASSE-SPLEEN

Arsac

CH. FOURCAS-DUPRE

D1

CH. FOURCAS-HOSTEN

Listrac-Medoc

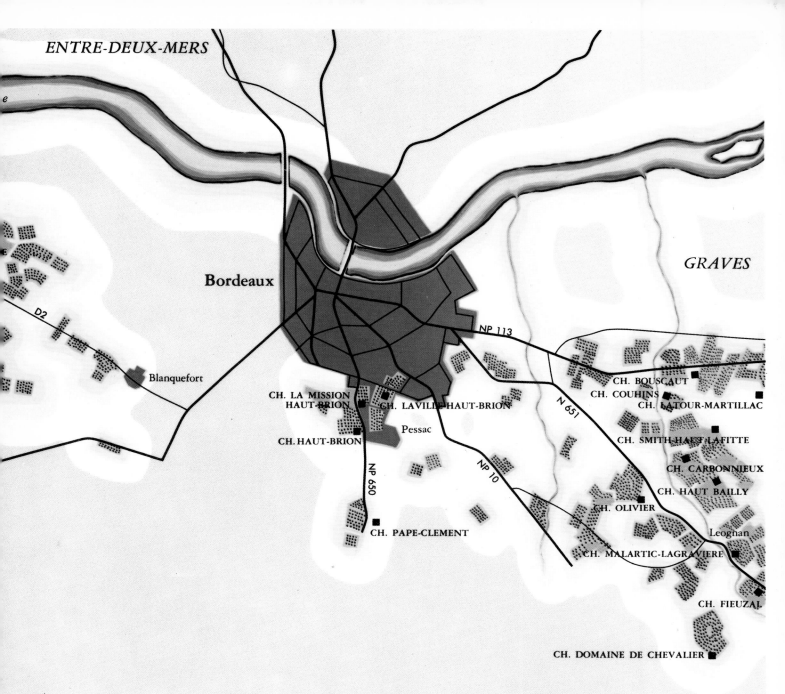

ENTRE-DEUX-MERS

Bordeaux

GRAVES

Blanquefort

D2

NP 113

CH. BOUSCAUT
CH. COUHINS
CH. LATOUR-MARTILLAC

N 651

CH. LA MISSION HAUT-BRION
CH. LAVILLE-HAUT-BRION

Pessac

CH. SMITH-HAUT-LAFITTE

CH. HAUT-BRION

CH. CARBONNIEUX

NP 650

NP 10

CH. HAUT BAILLY

CH. OLIVIER

Leognan

CH. PAPE-CLEMENT

CH. MALARTIC-LAGRAVIÈRE

CH. FIEUZAL

CH. DOMAINE DE CHEVALIER

Mis en Bouteille au Château
1971
Château Bouscaut
GRAND CRU CLASSÉ
1 PT. 8 FL OZS   ALCOHOL 12 °/. BY VOL.

APPELLATION GRAVES CONTROLEE
Domaine Wohlstetter - Sloan
Sté Civile du Château Bouscaut
PROPRIÉTAIRE
à CADAUJAC près BORDEAUX
RED BORDEAUX WINE   PRODUCT OF FRANCE

MIS EN BOUTEILLES AU CHÂTEAU

CHATEAU LAFITE-ROTHSCHILD
1961
APPELLATION PAUILLAC CONTRÔLÉE

CHATEAU
MALARTIC-LAGRAVIÈRE
Grand vin de Bordeaux
1967
CRU CLASSÉ DE GRAVES
APPELLATION GRAVES CONTRÔLÉE

JACQUES MARLY-RIDORET PROPRIÉTAIRE A LÉOGNAN (GIRONDE)
MISE EN BOUTEILLE AU CHATEAU

SAUTERNES AND BARSAC

CHATEAU
DE
RAYNE-VIGNEAU
MIS EN BOUTEILLE AU CHATEAU
1964
1ᵉʳ GRAND CRU
SAUTERNES
APPELLATION SAUTERNES CONTROLÉE
PRODUCE OF FRANCE   G. RAOUX · PROPRIÉTAIRE

N
W E
S

1 MILE

Barsac

Garonne

CH. COUTET

CH. CLIMENS

Préignac

N 113

Ciron

D 8

CH. RABAUD
PROMIS

CH. SUDUIRAUT

CH. RABAUD-SIGALAS

CH. LAFAURIE-PEYRAGUEY

CH. RAYNE-VIGNEAU

D 116

CH. HAUT-PEYRAGUEY

Langon

CH. D'YQUEM

CH. LA TOUR
BLANCHE

Sauternes

CH. RIEUSSEC

Fargues

CH. GUIRAUD

D 125

Saint-Estèphe. Some experts say that because the soil is different in the northern reaches of the Haut-Medoc, having more clay and less gravel, the wines of Saint-Estèphe tend to be firmer, higher in tannin content, and slower to mature than the other wines of the district. The wines of the leading vineyards are prized for their depth and sturdiness. They are dark, tannic wines, slow to offer up their bouquet and very long-lived.

RECOMMENDED ST.-ESTÈPHE WINES

Ch. Meyney	$3–$5
Ch. Marbuzet	$3–$5
Ch. Les Ormes de Pez	$3–$5
Ch. Phélan-Ségur	$3–$7
Ch. de Pez	$4–$7
Ch. Lafon-Rochet	$4–$8
Ch. Cos-Labory	$4–$8
Ch. Cos d'Estournel	$5–$10
Ch. Calon-Ségur	$5–$10
Ch. Montrose	$5–$10

Pauillac. South of the vineyards of Saint-Estèphe lies the Médoc's most distinguished commune, Pauillac. Three of the five First Growths are planted within its boundaries: Lafite-Rothschild, Latour, and Mouton-Rothschild. To many they represent the ideal claret: smooth but full-bodied, with great depth and also a hint of luscious fruit, having a tremendous fragrance that develops as they mature. Perfectly balanced, the wines have a subtlety and distinction all their own. When allowed to reach the lofty peak of greatness, each is literally beyond adequate description, offering a wine-drinking experience second to none. Unfortunately, most bottles of Lafite, Mouton, and Latour are consumed too young, as their purchasers these days frequently lack the patience to wait ten, fifteen, or twenty years for the wines to mature.

Though Lafite, Latour, and Mouton are certainly the most famous, many other fine vineyards lie within the confines of Pauillac.

RECOMMENDED PAUILLAC WINES

Ch. Grand-Puy-Ducasse	$3–$7
Ch. Grand-Puy-Lacoste	$4–$8
Ch. Pontet-Canet	$4–$8
Ch. Duhart-Milon-Rothschild	$4–$8
Ch. Clerc-Milon	$4–$8
Ch. Mouton-Baron-Philippe	$4–$8
Ch. Haut-Batailley	$4–$8
Ch. Lynch-Bages	$5–$10
Ch. Pichon-Longueville-Lalande	$5–$10
Ch. Pichon-Longueville	$5–$10
Ch. Lafite-Rothschild, Ch. Latour, Ch. Mouton-Rothschild	$10–$25

The cellar master watches over his wines fermenting in oak casks until they are ready for bottling

Saint-Julien. This commune produces superlative wines among the châteaus of the second, third, and fourth ranks. Lying between Pauillac and Margaux, Saint-Julien draws a bit from the style of each. Slightly fuller in body than a Margaux, the typical Saint-Julien bears more resemblance to some of the wines of Pauillac. Saint-Julien wines are relatively quick to mature and, like Margaux wines, have a rather tender quality that makes them highly desirable. While the name Pauillac rarely appears by itself on a label, since most of the vineyard lands belong to the important châteaus and there is little ground to cultivate for regional wine, the commune wines of Saint-Julien can be found more frequently, and generally can be counted on for excellent value.

RECOMMENDED ST.-JULIEN WINES

B&G St.-Julien	$5
Ch. Langoa-Barton	$3–$7
Ch. Gloria	$4–$8
Ch. Talbot	$4–$8
Ch. Beychevelle	$4–$8
Ch. Ducru-Beaucaillou	$4–$8
Ch. Gruaud-Larose	$4–$8
Ch. Léoville-Barton	$4–$8
Ch. Léoville-Las-Cases	$4–$8
Ch. Léoville-Poyferré	$4–$8

Margaux. The noble name Margaux sometimes leads to confusion, since it applies both to a commune and to a specific vineyard. Its greatest distinction derives from Château Margaux, a First Growth whose wines are noted for their exquisite breed, velvety texture, and richly haunting bouquet. These supple wines from the southernmost of the famous communes ripen early into suave and silky beauties possessing the floweriest fragrance of any wine from the Médoc. With much agreeable commune wine being rightfully sold under the name Margaux, the unwary buyer may take this to be the wine of the famous château. The considerable price difference, however, is a clue to the quality of the wines. Besides the marvelous wines of Château Margaux, several other outstanding wines from the commune command attention year after year.

RECOMMENDED MARGAUX WINES

Sichel Margaux	$5
Ch. Cantenac-Brown	$3–$7
Ch. Malescot-St.-Exupéry	$3–$7
Ch. Prieuré-Lichine	$3–$7
Ch. Kirwan	$3–$7
Ch. Brane-Cantenac	$3–$7
Ch. Lascombes	$4–$8
Ch. Giscours	$4–$8
Ch. Rauzan-Gassies	$4–$8
Ch. Rausan-Ségla	$4–$8
Ch. Palmer	$5–$10
Ch. Margaux	$10–$20

GREAT GROWTHS OF THE MÉDOC

In 1855 a selected group of Bordeaux wine authorities were requested to rank the very finest vineyards of the Médoc in five categories. Sixty-two vineyards won this elite standing. The judges also placed Château Haut-Brion of Graves in the top group, since they could not overlook its world-famous wine. The 1855 list of honor appears below, modified according to the French government's decree of June 21, 1973, granting a new official and legal classification to the First Growths of the red Médoc wines.

1855 Official Classification of the Great Growths of the Médoc as Amended in 1973

Château	Commune	Estimated Current Production in Cases	Comments
FIRST GROWTHS			
Lafite	Pauillac	25,000	Elegance and finesse; relatively light, owing to a high proportion of the Merlot grape. Great.
Latour	Pauillac	25,000	With a high Cabernet Sauvignon content, robust, deep, and full-bodied; a noble wine needing years to mature.
Margaux	Margaux	20,000	Elegant, suave, and delicate wine, certainly the most feminine of all the First Growths.
Mouton-Rothschild	Pauillac	25,000	Though not as delicate as Lafite, the wine has its own special depth and grandeur. Remarkable.
Haut-Brion (by assimilation)	Pessac	18,000	Very full and rich, even in years when lesser vineyards falter.
SECOND GROWTHS			
Rausan-Segla	Margaux	10,000	Fine and perfumed, a light and velvety wine.
Rauzan-Gassies	Margaux	8,000	Delicate, but a bit thin; the wine is no longer considered the equal of other Second Growths.
Léoville-Las-Cases	Saint-Julien	20,000	Excellent, justly famous wine, always full of flavor. Well-balanced.
Léoville-Poyferré	Saint-Julien	20,000	A worthy rival of Las-Cases, usually the fullest of the three Léovilles.
Léoville-Barton	Saint-Julien	15,000	A solid Second Growth, with good body in great vintages.
Durfort-Vivens	Margaux	7,500	A well-made wine, but often not so good as many others of this rank. Not prominent.
Gruaud-Larose	Saint-Julien	25,000	Popular, fruity, and fast-maturing.
Lascombes	Margaux	25,000	Now has the status of one of the best of the Second Growths. Exceptional bouquet and finesse.
Brane-Cantenac	Cantenac	25,000	Big and dependable, but sometimes coarse. Not one of the leaders.
Pichon-Longueville-Baron	Pauillac	18,000	A consistent, rich, and powerful wine.
Pichon-Lalande	Pauillac	20,000	Suppler and lighter than the other Pichon.
Ducru-Beaucaillou	Saint-Julien	15,000	Now manifesting the full richness afforded by its pebbly soil.
Cos d'Estournel	Saint-Estèphe	25,000	Lighter than other wines of this commune, but still full, fine, and sturdy.
Montrose	Saint-Estèphe	25,000	Relatively hard, extremely long-lived. Popular in England.
THIRD GROWTHS			
Kirwan	Margaux	10,000	Improved, but no longer of Third Growth status.
Issan	Margaux	10,000	A rich, proud, and typically delicate Margaux wine.
Lagrange	Saint-Julien	22,000	Coarse and slow-maturing, not the equal of most of the other Third Growths.
Langoa-Barton	Saint-Julien	15,000	Good, typical Saint-Julien, lighter than its Léoville neighbor.

Château	Commune	Estimated Current Production in Cases	Comments
Giscours	Labarde	25,000	Delicate and improved; now rather popular.
Malescot-Saint-Exupéry	Margaux	10,000	Elegant and richly bouqueted, a sound Third Growth.
Cantenac-Brown	Cantenac	10,000	Big, strong, and improving, the wine still deserves its rank.
La Lagune	Ludon	25,000	Slow to mature, with a bit of the taste of the wines from Graves. Perhaps deserves a higher rank.
Palmer	Margaux	17,000	Elegant, good bouquet; highest-priced except for First Growths.
Desmirail	Margaux	—	No longer exists; has been absorbed by its neighbor Palmer.
Calon-Ségur	Saint-Estèphe	22,000	With Montrose, possibly the most robust and long-lived of the Saint-Estèphes.
Ferrière	Margaux	—	No longer exists; has been absorbed by its neighbor Lascombes.
Marquis d'Alesme Becker	Margaux	5,000	Not well-known; a minor wine no longer of Third Growth status.
Boyd-Cantenac	Cantenac	5,000	Light and well-made, but little-known.

FOURTH GROWTHS

Château	Commune	Estimated Current Production in Cases	Comments
Saint-Pierre	Saint-Julien	10,000	Sound, light, not overly interesting wine. Hard to find. (In 1855 called Saint Pierre Bontemps and Saint Pierre-Sevaistre.)
Talbot	Saint-Julien	30,000	Dependable, big, and fruity wine that might even deserve a higher rank.
Branaire-Ducru	Saint-Julien	15,000	An uneven wine, but one that has lately shown improvement.
Duhart-Milon	Pauillac	15,000	A wine to watch, now often as good as some Second Growths.
Pouget	Margaux	5,000	The lesser wine of Boyd-Cantenac. Not of great distinction.
La Tour-Carnet	Saint-Laurent	10,000	Obscure and unexceptional in recent years; in 1966 its return to excellence began.
Lafon-Rochet	Saint-Estèphe	15,000	Won an award as the best of the great 1970 Saint-Estèphes. Happy harmony of the long-lived hardness of Saint-Estèphe and the complexity of Pauillac, which it borders.
Beychevelle	Saint-Julien	25,000	Very elegant, popular Médoc, worthy of Second Growth rank.
Prieuré-Lichine	Cantenac	20,000	Elegant, flavorful and fast-maturing, the wine can challenge many a Second Growth.
Marquis-de-Terme	Margaux	20,000	One of the better of its class; rich and full.

FIFTH GROWTHS

Château	Commune	Estimated Current Production in Cases	Comments
Pontet-Canet	Pauillac	40,000	Largest single classified vineyard of the Médoc. Opposite Mouton-Rothschild, but the wine is a bit lighter.
Batailley	Pauillac	20,000	Good average quality, but not distinguished.

Château	Commune	Estimated Current Production in Cases	Comments
Haut-Batailley	Pauillac	10,000	Until 1942 part of Batailley. The wines are similar in characteristics.
Grand-Puy-Lacoste	Pauillac	15,000	Excellent, dependable wine deserving a higher rank.
Grand-Puy-Ducasse	Pauillac	10,000	Has less body than Grand-Puy-Lacoste. Finesse.
Lynch-Bages	Pauillac	22,000	Rich, concentrated. Often called "the poor man's Mouton-Rothschild" because of its power and depth.
Lynch-Moussas	Pauillac	10,000	Like the above château, once the property of an Irish Mayor of Bordeaux named Lynch. The wine is well known in the Low Countries but almost unheard-of in Britain and the United States. Not long-lived.
Dauzac	Labarde-Margaux	15,000	Until recently rather undistinguished, but projects a better future.
Mouton-Baron-Philippe	Pauillac	15,000	Can be considered a lighter version of the famous Mouton-Rothschild. The estates are adjacent and have the same proprietor.
du Tertre	Arsac-Margaux	15,000	Acceptable wine, without the majesty of the other classified growths.
Haut-Bages-Libéral	Pauillac	10,000	Full, powerful, and improving.
Pédesclaux	Pauillac	6,000	Obscure, far from outstanding.
Belgrave	Saint-Laurent	15,000	Full, fruity, but varies from year to year.
Camensac	Saint-Laurent	12,000	Pleasant but lacking in distinction.
Cos Labory	Saint-Estèphe	7,500	Like other Saint-Estèphes, big and long-lived.
Clerc-Milon	Pauillac	8,000	Full and rich, now one of the holdings of the Mouton-Rothschild *domaine*.
Croizet-Bages	Pauillac	10,000	Good, but not outstanding.
Cantemerle	Macau	15,000	Very fine and light, with an excellent bouquet; should have a higher rating.

The Médoc châteaus listed below in alphabetical order have shown so much merit during recent decades that in our opinion they are worthy of being considered the equals of the Fifth Growths of the original 1855 classification.

Recommended Additions (as of 1977) to the Official Classification

Château	Commune	Estimated Current Production in Cases	Comments
Angludet	Margaux	10,000	Light and very supple; quite an engaging wine.
Bel-Air-Marquis-d'Aligre	Margaux	10,000	Consistently exhibits the finesse and delicacy associated with Margaux wines.
Chasse-Spleen	Moulis	20,000	Exceptional wine has been produced since the mid-1950s.
Fourcas-Dupré	Listrac	10,000	Full, long-lived.
Fourcas-Hosten	Listrac	12,000	Rich, even, and well-balanced.
Gloria	Saint-Julien	17,000	Similar in style to Léoville-Poyferré, and almost its equal.
de Pez	Saint-Estèphe	13,000	Directly opposite Calon-Ségur; the wine has the same depth and excellence.
Phélan-Ségur	Saint-Estèphe	20,000	With the richness, tannin, and depth typically associated with Saint-Estèphe.
Siran	Margaux	7,000	Much improved. Softly perfumed.

GRAVES

South and west of the city of Bordeaux lie the vineyards of Graves, originally known for their white wines. But the reds have long since come into their own, gaining the attention and acclaim they deserve. Though they do resemble certain Médocs, Graves red wines tend to be sturdier, asserting themselves with an appealing forthrightness.

The white wines of Graves are somewhat less distinguished than the reds, though some châteaus with high standards produce a light, pleasantly dry white wine (often in vintages that were poor for red wines). However, a great deal of white Graves, sold simply as Graves, is rather thin, sweetish, and undistinguished.

RECOMMENDED GRAVES WINES

Red		White	
Ch. Haut-Bailly	$3–$7	Ch. Couhins	$3–$5
Ch. Malartic-Lagravière	$3–$7	Ch. Malartie-Lagravière	$3–$5
Ch. Bouscaut	$4–$8	Ch. Olivier	$3–$5
Ch. Pape-Clément	$4–$8	Ch. Latour-Martillac	$3–$5
Ch. Domaine de Chevalier	$4–$8	Ch. Carbonnieux	$3–$5
Ch. La Tour-Haut-Brion	$4–$8	Ch. Bouscaut Blanc	$5–$7
Ch. La Mission Haut-Brion	$5–$10	Ch. Laville-Haut-Brion	$5–$8
Ch. Haut-Brion	$10–$20	Ch. Haut-Brion	$15–$20

SAINT-ÉMILION

The wines of Saint-Émilion are known for their generous nature—perhaps the most generous of all Bordeaux. Robust, warm-hearted wines, they are attractive even when drunk young. Their full and savory character has led them to be called "the Burgundies of Bordeaux" (though neither the Burgundians nor the Bordelais approve of the expression, it nevertheless contains some truth). The two greatest wines of Saint-Émilion, Cheval Blanc and Ausone, are in a class by themselves, ranking with the four top Médocs, Haut-Brion of Graves, and Petrus of Pomerol as the most remarkable wines of Bordeaux.

Because they are fruity and quick to mature, Saint-Émilions are often in youth the most attractive of the red Bordeaux. Saint-Émilion regional wines are especially attractive during their younger years.

RECOMMENDED ST.-ÉMILION WINES

Sichel St. Émilion	$4	Ch. La Gaffelière	$4–$8
Ch. Chauvin	$3–$5	Ch. Figeac	$4–$8
Ch. Dassault	$3–$5	Ch. Beauséjour	$4–$8
Ch. Ripeau	$3–$5	Ch. l'Angélus	$4–$8
Ch. Tertre-Daugay	$3–$5	Ch. Troplong-Mondot	$4–$8
Ch. Belair	$3–$6	Clos. Fourtet	$5–$10
Ch. Canon	$3–$6	Ch. Magdelaine	$5–$10
Ch. Pavie	$3–$6	Ch. Ausone, Ch. Cheval Blanc	$10–$20
Ch. Trottevieille	$3–$6		

POMEROL

Adjoining Saint-Émilion is Pomerol, the smallest district in Bordeaux. Its fruity wines mature even earlier than the Saint-Émilions. As in several of the other regions of Bordeaux, liberal use of the Merlot grape imparts softness and delicacy to the wines.

In poor years some Pomerols can be quite good, maintaining a remarkable continuity of gentle roundness and ripe scent.

RECOMMENDED POMEROL WINES

Ch. Gazin	$4–$7	Ch. Clinet	$4–$7
Ch. Lafleur	$4–$7	Ch. Lagrange	$4–$7
Ch. Nénin	$4–$7	Ch. La Fleur-Petrus	$5–$8
Ch. Petit-Village	$4–$7	Ch. La Conseillante	$5–$8
Ch. Rouget	$4–$7	Ch. Latour-à-Pomerol	$5–$8
Ch. Trotanoy	$4–$7	Ch. Petrus	$10–$30
Vieux-Château-Certan	$4–$7		

SAUTERNES AND BARSAC

Sauternes, the fifth of the districts that lend great distinction to the region of Bordeaux, produces the luscious, fruity, and dramatic sweet white wine acclaimed everywhere.

Making Sauternes is extremely costly, and only the best châteaus can afford to do it properly. Beginning in October, the pickers go into the vineyards to clip, one by one, those clusters of grapes that have been attacked by the dusty mold *Botrytis cinerea*. This special fungus, developing fully only in great vintages, transforms the grapes from a state of complete ripeness to one of *pourriture noble,* or "noble rot." The botrytis allows the water in the grapes to escape, leaving in its wake a rich concentration of fruit, sugar, and natural acids. The tedious method of harvesting, repeated as many as eight or nine times, weather permitting, may continue in a fine year into December, until the last grape has succumbed to the fungus and then to the field hand's knife. More than in any other Bordeaux wine district, the success of the wine of Sauternes depends on the weather. In poor years (of which there have been many in the last decade), either the vineyards produce no Sauternes worthy of the name or the grapes are vinified into an undistinguished dry white wine.

At the head of the ranking of Sauternes wines stands Château d'Yquem. Its magnificence is not exaggerated: superb, smooth sweetness, almost creamy but never cloying, utterly luscious fruit, and a rich perfume redolent of flowers and spices. No true wine lover should deny himself the exquisite pleasure that this rich, golden wine of Sauternes affords. But be forewarned not to chill it into numbness. Severe cold can mask a multitude of sins in an inferior wine, but fine Sauternes has nothing to hide, and every nuance should be enjoyed.

RECOMMENDED SAUTERNES AND BARSAC WINES

Ch. Guiraud	$3–$7	Ch. Climens	$4–$8
Ch. La Tour Blanche	$3–$7	Ch. Coutet	$4–$8
Ch. Suduiraut	$3–$7	Ch. d'Yquem	$10–$25
Ch. Rieussec	$3–$7		

Claret bottles resting on their sides form a brilliant honeycomb pattern

BURGUNDY

Burgundies are big wines, fat with "stuffing," heady with perfume, round and full and deep in all respects. Hugh Johnson has aptly observed, "Bordeaux appeals to the aesthete as Burgundy appeals to the sensualist." Exposed to the air, Burgundies unfold their complexities assertively, revealing a tremendous power and concentrated richness with an authority that earns them the title "King of Wines." Delicate they can be, especially in texture, and sometimes in bouquet and fruit. Some are as elegant as classic claret; many deserve to be called noble.

Burgundy proper and its neighboring vineyards stretch some 130 miles south from Dijon, a city in earlier times more famous for its wine than for its mustard. The first section is by far the most important: the Côte d'Or, whose renowned vineyards include two subdistricts, the Côte de Nuits to the north and the Côte de Beaune to the south. Below the town of Chagny lie the lesser districts of Burgundy, the Côte Chalonnaise and the Mâconnais. Finally, there are the hills of Beaujolais, home of that high-spirited and delightful young wine.

Burgundy produces less than one-third the volume of wine that Bordeaux does. The fine and famous wines of the Côte d'Or make up only 5 percent of the total. Scarce and expensive, these superb wines can only become more so in the face of ever-increasing demand. In order to buy intelligently, one must have a thorough knowledge not only of the communes and vineyards, as in Bordeaux, but also of the individual growers' parcels of a particular vineyard, for some growers take greater pains than others in making their wines. Among the vineyard

The Pinot Noir is the great grape of Burgundy and Champagne, producing all the best red Burgundies and two-thirds of the champagne

Facing: The Cadets de Bourgogne, a prankish glee club whose forte is drinking songs, amuse their fellow members of the Chevaliers du Tastevin. Their maxim: "Wine is good for women—when men drink it."
© Arnold Newman

owners with reputations are the following, and any of these names on a Burgundy label is an assurance of a quality wine: Claude Ramonet, Duc de Magenta, Comte de Vogüé, Bonneau Martray, René Engel, Gros, Comte Lafon, Armand Rousseau, Domaine de la Romanée-Conti, Jayer, Henri Lamarche, Jean Grivot, Clair-Daü, Pierre Matrot, Étienne Sauzet, Marquis d'Angerville, Roland Thévenin, J. Faiveley.

The *Appellation Contrôlée* laws in Burgundy are more complex than in any other region. Yet in a way they are more useful, since the laws single out the names of the very best vineyards. Each of the top thirty-one vineyards has been granted its own *Appellation*—Musigny, Clos de Vougeot, Bonnes-Mares, Chambertin, Richebourg, Montrachet, and so on. These *Grand Cru* vineyards need not identify even the name of the village in which they are located. In fact, many villages have appended their most illustrious vineyard's name to their own. Thus Chambolle is now Chambolle-Musigny, Gevrey is Gevrey-Chambertin, and Aloxe is Aloxe-Corton. This practice can lead to the same sort of confusion as was pointed out in connection with the name Margaux in Bordeaux: a buyer who does not know better may think he is getting the great Chambertin when he buys the village wine called Gevrey-Chambertin—which, however, may be quite good.

Wines of the second level, comparable to a classified Second or Third Growth of the Médoc, are designated as *Premier Cru*. Their legal *Appellation* consists of the commune name followed by the name of a specific vineyard. With the wine called Volnay-Caillerets, for example, Volnay is the name of the village, Caillerets the name of one of its best vineyards. When the village name appears alone with the words *Premier Cru*, it usually means that the wine comes from more than one of the *Premier Cru* vineyards.

The *Appellation Contrôlée* laws also limit the grape varieties which may be planted. For red wines, only the Pinot Noir is permitted. For whites, Pinot Chardonnay predominates, though a little Pinot Blanc is planted here and there. The maximum yield per acre is regulated as well—the better the vineyard, the smaller the crop. A fine Burgundian winemaker will estate-bottle his vintages. When the words *Mis en bouteilles à la Propriété, Mise au Domaine,* or *Mis en bouteilles au Domaine* appear on the label, they guarantee that the wine was made and bottled by the grower and is genuinely what the label represents it to be.

A phrase that appears very often on corks and labels is *Mis en bouteilles dans nos Caves,* or "Bottled in our cellars." The cellars are usually those of a shipper. If the wine is not bottled by the grower himself, he traditionally sells his wine to one of these shippers, or *négociants*—who may or may not handle the wine scrupulously. Most of the shippers in Burgundy have high standards and produce superb wines; others, unfortunately, do not. One needs to know something of their reputations in order to be able to choose intelligently. Many of the great Burgundy houses have contributed to the honor of the trade for centuries and themselves own sections of the top vineyards. One can generally be certain of getting good wines from such shippers as Joseph Drouhin, Louis Latour, and Louis Jadot. Other well-respected shippers are Bouchard Père et Fils, Remoissenet, Patriarche, Chanson, Faiveley, Mommessin, Thorin, Leroy, and Moillard.

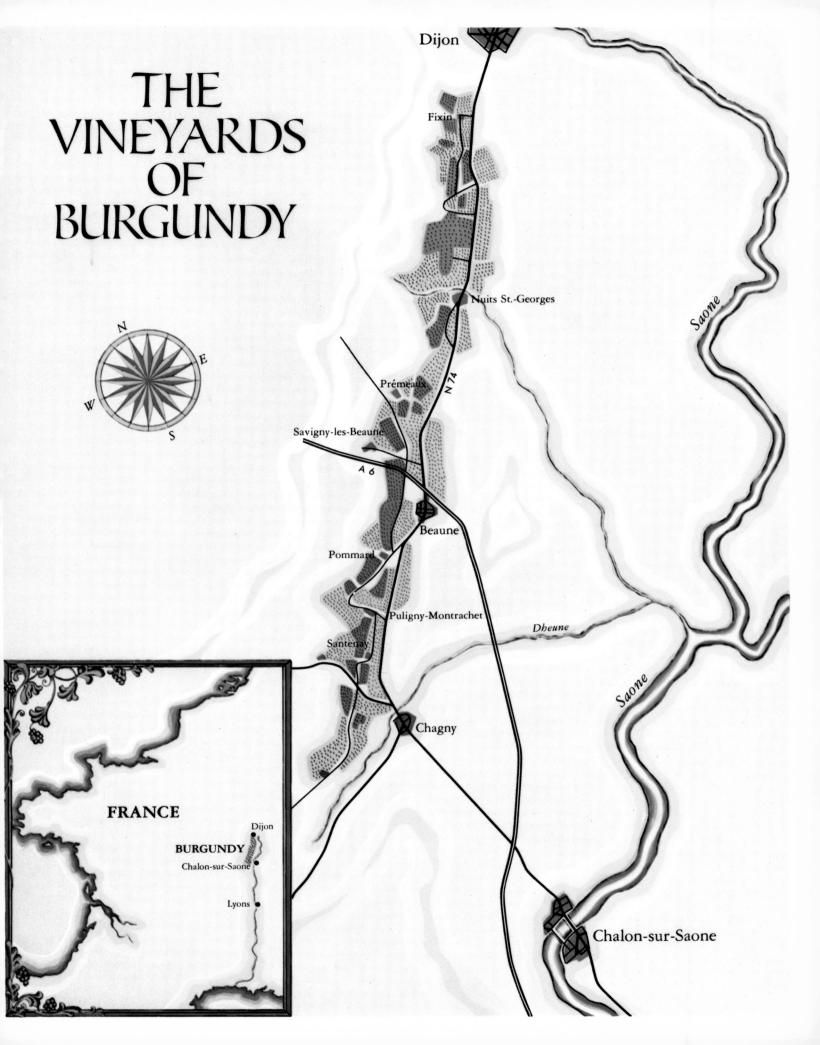

THE
VINEYARDS
OF
BURGUNDY

N
W · E
S

Dijon

Fixin

Nuits St.-Georges

Prémeaux

N 74

Savigny-les-Beaune

A 6

Beaune

Pommard

Puligny-Montrachet

Dheune

Santenay

Saone

Saone

Chagny

FRANCE

Dijon

BURGUNDY

Chalon-sur-Saone

Lyons

Chalon-sur-Saone

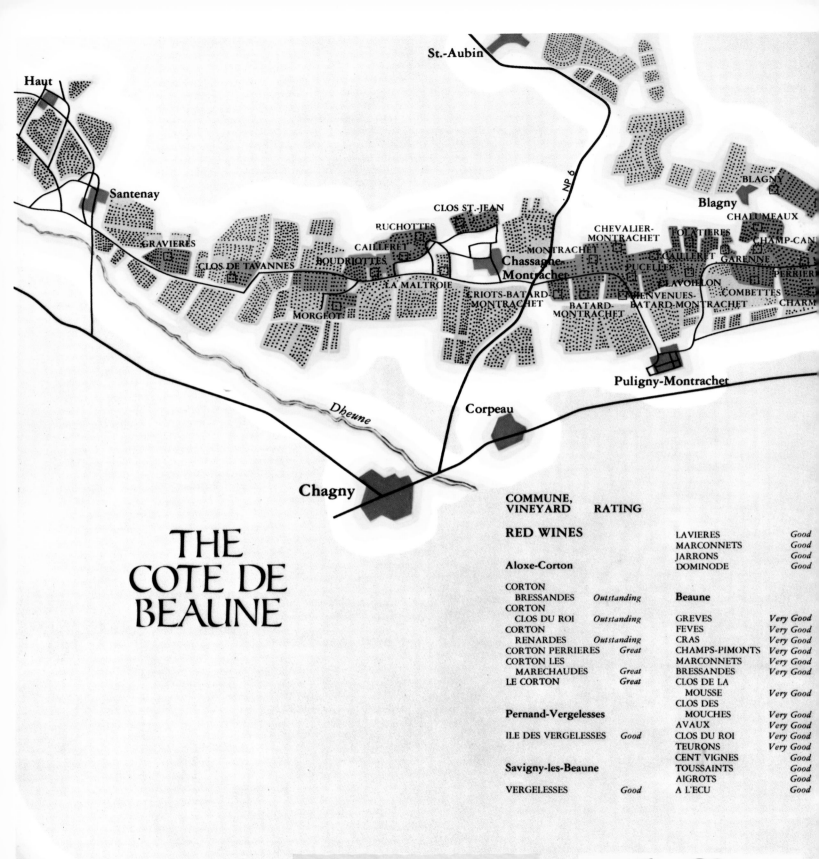

St.-Aubin

Haut

Santenay

GRAVIERES

CLOS DE TAVANNES

BOUDRIOTTES

MORGEOT

LA MALTROIE

CAILLERET

RUCHOTTES

CLOS ST.-JEAN

MONTRACHET

Chassagne-Montrachet

CRIOTS-BATARD-MONTRACHET

BATARD-MONTRACHET

CHEVALIER-MONTRACHET

PUCELLES

CLAVOILLON

BIENVENUES-BATARD-MONTRACHET

FOLATIERES

CAILLERET

GARENNE

COMBETTES

BLAGNY

Blagny

CHALUMEAUX

CHAMP-CAN

PERRIER

CHARM

Puligny-Montrachet

Corpeau

Dheune

Chagny

NP 6

THE CÔTE DE BEAUNE

COMMUNE, VINEYARD	RATING
RED WINES	
Aloxe-Corton	
CORTON BRESSANDES	*Outstanding*
CORTON CLOS DU ROI	*Outstanding*
CORTON RENARDES	*Outstanding*
CORTON PERRIERES	*Great*
CORTON LES MARECHAUDES	*Great*
LE CORTON	*Great*
Pernand-Vergelesses	
ILE DES VERGELESSES	*Good*
Savigny-les-Beaune	
VERGELESSES	*Good*

	RATING
LAVIERES	*Good*
MARCONNETS	*Good*
JARRONS	*Good*
DOMINODE	*Good*
Beaune	
GREVES	*Very Good*
FEVES	*Very Good*
CRAS	*Very Good*
CHAMPS-PIMONTS	*Very Good*
MARCONNETS	*Very Good*
BRESSANDES	*Very Good*
CLOS DE LA MOUSSE	*Very Good*
CLOS DES MOUCHES	*Very Good*
AVAUX	*Very Good*
CLOS DU ROI	*Very Good*
TEURONS	*Very Good*
CENT VIGNES	*Good*
TOUSSAINTS	*Good*
AIGROTS	*Good*
A L'ECU	*Good*

1972

Blagny
.La Pièce sous le Bois.
APPELLATION CONTROLÉE
Domaine Joseph Matrot
Propriétaire à Meursault (Côte d'Or)
Alcohol by vol. 12°

Joseph Drouhin
WHITE BURGUNDY TABLE WINE   ALCOHOL BY VOLUME 12°   PRODUCT OF FRANCE   CONT. 1 PINT 8 FL. OZS

MEURSAULT-PERRIÈRES

APPELLATION CONTROLÉE

MIS EN BOUTEILLE PAR
JOSEPH DROUHIN
Maison fondée en 1880
NÉGOCIANT A BEAUNE, CÔTE-D'OR
AUX CELLIERS DES ROIS DE FRANCE ET DES DUCS DE BOURGOGNE

AGENT   Dreyfus Ashby & Co   NEW YORK, N.Y.

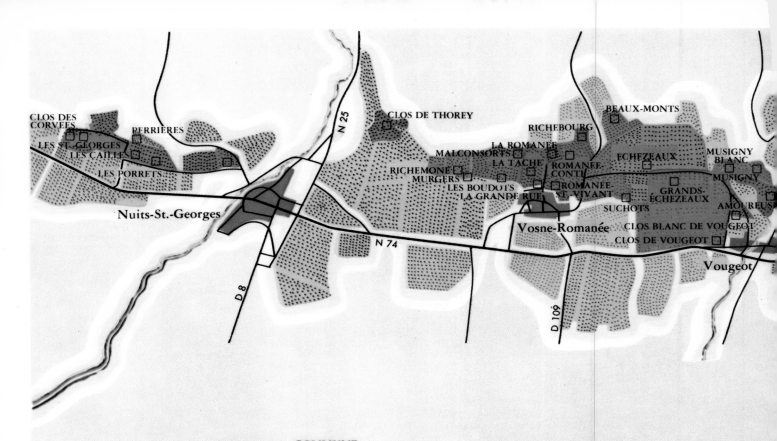

THE COTE DE NUITS

COMMUNE, VINEYARD — RATING

RED WINES

Fixin

LES HERVELETS	Very Good
CLOS DU CHAPITRE	Very Good
CLOS DE LA PERRIERE	Very Good
ARVELETS	Very Good
CLOS NAPOLEON	Very Good

• Gevrey-Chambertin

CHAMBERTIN	Outstanding
CLOS DE BEZE	Outstanding
LATRICIERES-CHAMBERTIN	Great
MAZIS-CHAMBERTIN	Great
CHARMES-CHAMBERTIN	Great
MAZOYERES-CHAMBERTIN	Great
GRIOTTE-CHAMBERTIN	Great
RUCHOTTES-CHAMBERTIN	Great
CHAPELLE-CHAMBERTIN	Great
CLOS ST.-JACQUES	Great

Morey-St.-Denis

BONNES MARES	Outstanding
CLOS DE LA ROCHE	Great
CLOS DE TART	Very Good
CLOS ST.-DENIS	Very Good
CLOS DES LAMBRAYS	Very Good

Chambolle-Musigny

MUSIGNY	Outstanding
BONNES MARES	Outstanding
AMOUREUSES	Great
CHARMES	Very Good

Vougeot

CLOS DE VOUGEOT	Outstanding

Flagey-Echezeaux

GRANDS-ECHEZEAUX	Outstanding
ECHEZEAUX	Very Good

Vosne-Romanée

ROMANEE-CONTI	Outstanding
LA TACHE	Outstanding
ROMANEE-ST.-VIVANT	Outstanding
RICHEBOURG	Outstanding
LA GRANDE RUE	Outstanding
LA ROMANEE	Great
MALCONSORTS	Great
SUCHOTS	Great
BEAUX-MONTS	Great

Nuits St.-Georges

LES ST.-GEORGES	Great
LES CAILLES	Great
CLOS DES CORVEES	Great
LES VAUCRAINS	Great

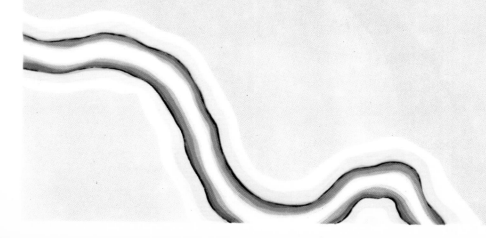

CHAMBERTIN CLOS DE BÈZE

APPELLATION CONTRÔLÉE

Domaine Armand Rousseau Père et Fils

GEVREY-CHAMBERTIN (CÔTE D'OR)

MISE AU DOMAINE   Product of France

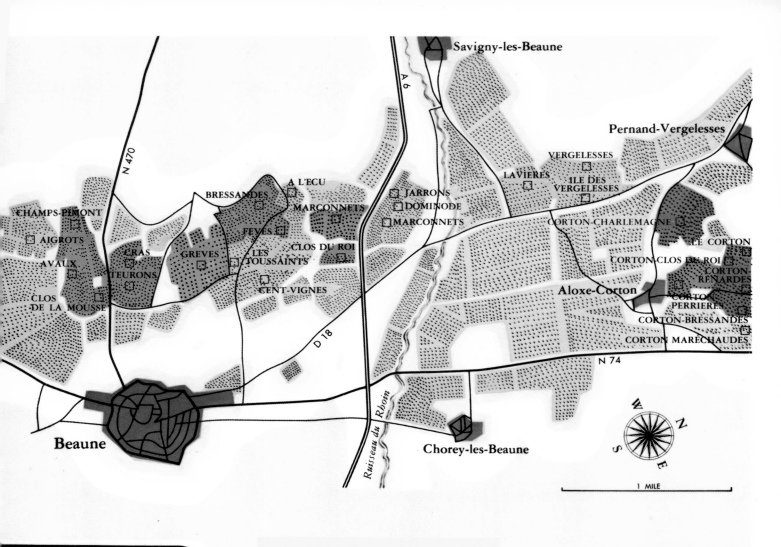

Savigny-les-Beaune

Pernand-Vergelesses

VERGELESSES

LAVIÈRES
ILE DES
VERGELESSES

CHAMPS-PIMONT

A L'ECU

BRESSANDES

JARRONS

DOMINODE

MARCONNETS

MARCONNETS

CORTON-CHARLEMAGNE

LE CORTON

AIGROTS

FEVES

CORTON-CLOS DU ROI

CRAS

GREVES

CLOS DU ROI

CORTON
RENARDES

AVAUX

TEURONS

LES
TOUSSAINTS

Aloxe-Corton

CORTON
PERRIÈRES

CLOS
DE LA MOUSSE

CENT-VIGNES

CORTON-BRESSANDES

CORTON MARÉCHAUDES

N 470

D 18

N 74

Ruisseau du Rhoin

Beaune

Chorey-les-Beaune

1 MILE

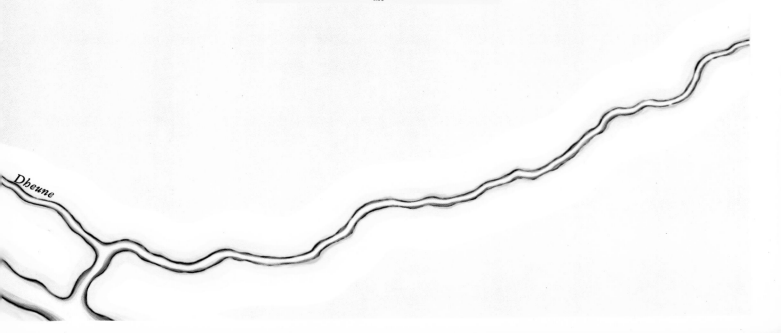

VOLNAY

APPELLATION D'ORIGINE CONTROLÉE

Clos des Chênes

RÉCOLTE DU DOMAINE PARENT

MIS EN BOUTEILLES PAR

JACQUES PARENT

JACQUES PARENT & Cⁱᵉ, NÉGOCIANTS A POMMARD, COTE-D'OR, FRANCE

CORTON

APPELLATION CONTROLÉE

Bonneau du Martray

PROPRIÉTAIRE A PERNAND-VERGELESSES & ALOXE-CORTON (COTE-D'OR)

Mis en bouteille
au Domaine

1973

PRODUCE OF FRANCE
0.73 L

Dheune

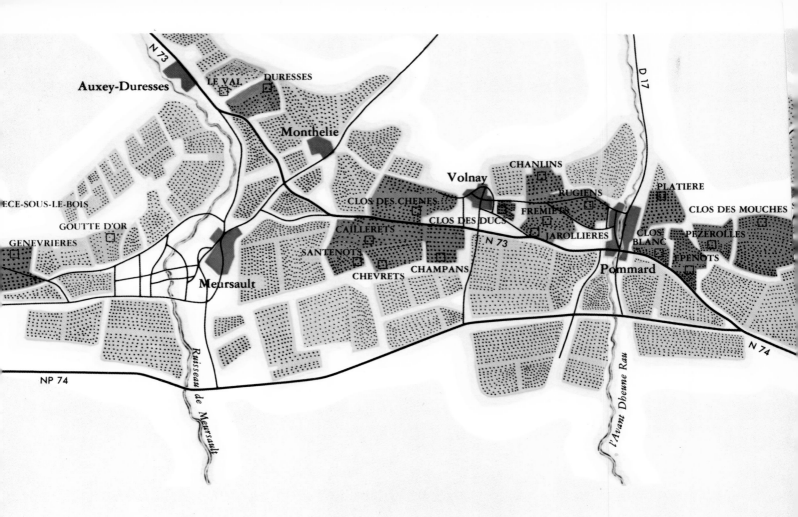

Map labels (top to bottom, left to right):

N 73 · D 17

Auxey-Duresses · LE VAL · DURESSES

Monthelie

CHANLINS

Volnay · RUGIENS · PLATIERE

ECE-SOUS-LE-BOIS · CLOS DES CHENES · FREMIETS · CLOS DES MOUCHES

GOUTTE D'OR · CLOS DES DUCS · JAROLLIERES · PEZEROLLES

GENEVRIERES · CAILLERETS · CLOS BLANC · EPENOTS

SANTENOTS · CHAMPANS · Pommard

Meursault · CHEVRETS

Ruisseau de Meursault · N 73 · N 74

NP 74 · l'Avant Dheune Rau

---

mmard			Chassagne-Montrachet			Meursault			PUCELLES	Great
GIENS	Great		BOUDRIOTTES	Very Good		PERRIERES	Great		CAILLERET	Great
ENOTS	Great		CLOS ST.-JEAN	Very Good		GENEVRIERES	Great		CHAMP-CANET	Very Good
ZEROLLES	Very Good		MALTROIE	Good		CHARMES	Great		GARENNE	Very Good
OS BLANC	Very Good		MORGEOT	Very Good		LA PIECE-SOUS-				
ANLINS	Very Good					LE-BOIS	Very Good		**Chassagne-Montrachet**	
ATIERE	Very Good					BLAGNY	Very Good			
ROLLIERES	Very Good		**Santenay**			SANTENOTS	Very Good		MONTRACHET	Outstanding
						GOUTTE D'OR	Good		BATARD-	
lnay			GRAVIÈRES	Very Good					MONTRACHET	Outstanding
			CLOS DE						CRIOTS-BATARD-	
OS DES DUCS	Great		TAVANNES	Very Good		**Puligny-Montrachet**			MONTRACHET	Outstanding
ILLERETS	Great								RUCHOTTES	Great
AMPANS	Great		**WHITE WINES**			MONTRACHET	Outstanding		MORGEOT	Very Good
EMIETS	Very Good					CHEVALIER-				
EVRETS	Very Good		**Aloxe-Corton**			MONTRACHET	Outstanding			
NTENOTS	Very Good					BATARD-				
OS DES			CORTON-			MONTRACHET	Outstanding			
CHENES	Very Good		CHARLEMAGNE	Outstanding		BIENVENUES-BATARD-				
						MONTRACHET	Outstanding			
xey			**Beaune**			COMBETTES	Great			
						CHALUMEAUX	Great			
RESSES	Very Good		CLOS DES			FOLATIERES	Great			
VAL	Good		MOUCHES	Very Good		CLAVOILLON	Very Good			

Outstanding Vineyard

Great Vineyard

Very Good Vineyard

Good Vineyard

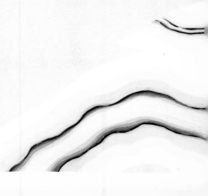

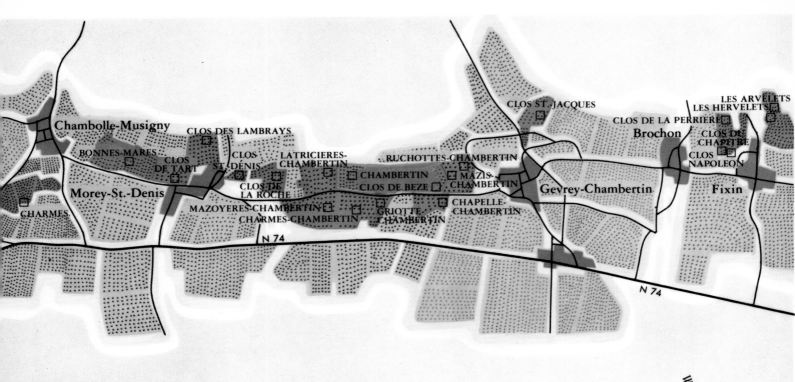

Chambolle-Musigny
CLOS DES LAMBRAYS
BONNES-MARES · CLOS DE TART · CLOS ST.-DÉNIS
CLOS · LATRICIERES-CHAMBERTIN · RUCHOTTES-CHAMBERTIN · CLOS ST.-JACQUES
CLOS DE LA PERRIERE
LES ARVELETS
LES HERVELETS
Brochon
CLOS DE CHAPITRE
CLOS NAPOLEON
CHAMBERTIN · MAZIS-CHAMBERTIN
Morey-St.-Denis · CLOS DE LA ROCHE · CLOS DE BEZE · Gevrey-Chambertin · Fixin
CHARMES · MAZOYERES-CHAMBERTIN · GRIOTTE-CHAMBERTIN · CHAPELLE-CHAMBERTIN
CHARMES-CHAMBERTIN
N 74
N 74

LES PRULIERS	Great	
LES PORRETS	Great	Outstanding Vineyard
CLOS DE THOREY	Great	Great Vineyard
LES BOUDOTS	Great	
MURGERS	Very Good	Very Good Vineyard
RICHEMONE	Very Good	Good Vineyard

WHITE WINES

Chambolle-Musigny

MUSIGNY BLANC   *Outstanding*

Vougeot

CLOS BLANC DE
VOUGEOT   *Great*

Nuits St.-Georges

PERRIERE   *Good*

RECOMMENDED CÔTE DE NUITS WINES

Red

Côte de Nuits Villages	$3–$6
Fixin	$4–$7
Clos Napoléon	$4–$7
Clos de la Perrière	$4–$7
Gevrey-Chambertin	$4–$8
Clos St. Jacques	$5–$8
Varoilles	$5–$8
Aux Combottes	$5–$8
Chapelle-Chambertin,	
Charmes Chambertin,	
Latricières-Chambertin,	
Ruchottes-Chambertin,	
Mazys-Chambertin,	
Mazoyères-Chambertin,	
Griotte-Chambertin	$7–$10
Le Chambertin, Chambertin-	
Clos de Bèze	$10–$20
Morey-St.-Denis	$4–$7
Clos de la Roche	$6–$10
Clos des Lambrays	$6–$10
Clos de Tart	$6–$10
Bonnes-Mares	$10–$20
Chambolle-Musigny	$4–$8
Amoureuses	$5–$9
Charmes	$5–$9
Bonnes-Mares	$10–$20
Vougeot	$4–$7
Clos de Vougeot	$10–$20
Vosne-Romanée	$4–$8
Malconsorts	$5–$8
Suchots	$5–$8
Grande Rue	$10–$20
La Romanée	$10–$20
Échezeaux	$10–$20
Romanée-St. Vivant,	
Grands-Échezeaux,	
La Tâche, Richebourg,	
Romanée-Conti	$15–$50
Nuits-St.-Georges	$4–$8
Les St. Georges	$5–$9
Porrets	$4–$8
Vaucrains	$4–$8
Pruliers	$4–$8

RECOMMENDED CÔTE DE BEAUNE WINES

White

Aloxe-Corton	
Corton-Charlemagne	$15–$20
Beaune	
Clos des Mouches Blanc	$7–$10
Meursault	$5–$8
Genevrières	$6–$10
Charmes	$6–$10
Goutte d'Or	$6–$10
Casse-Tête	$6–$10
Perrières	$6–$10
Auxey-Duresses	$3–$5
Monthélie	$3–$5
Puligny-Montrachet	$6–$10
Pucelles	$7–$11
Cailleret	$7–$11
Combettes	$7–$11
Referts	$7–$11
Bienvenues-Bâtard-	
Montrachet, Chevalier-	
Montrachet	$12–$20
Montrachet	$15–$30
Chassagne-Montrachet	$5–$9
Ruchottes	$6–$10
Caillerets	$6–$10
Boudriottes	$7–$11
Criots-Bâtard-Montrachet	$12–$20
Montrachet	$15–$30

Red

Côte de Beaune Villages	$3–$6
Auxey-Duresses	$4–$6
Aloxe-Corton	$5–$8
Corton-Grancey	$6–$10
Clos du Roi	$6–$10
Corton	$10–$20
Pernand-Vergelesses	$4–$6
Savigny-les-Beaune	$4–$6
Beaune	$4–$7
Grèves	$5–$8
Fèves	$5–$8
Cras	$5–$8
Clos des Mouches	$5–$10
Pommard	$5–$8

99

Rugiens	$6–$10	Pouilly-Loché	$3–$5
Épenots	$6–$10	Pouilly-Fuissé	$4–$7
Volnay	$5–$8		
Caillerets	$5–$10		
Clos des Chènes	$5–$10		
Clos des Ducs	$5–$10		

RECOMMENDED BEAUJOLAIS WINES

Red

Beaujolais	$2–$4
Beaujolais Villages	$3–$5
Morgon, Brouilly, Côte de Brouilly, Fleurie, Chénas, Chiroubles, Moulin à Vent, St.-Amour, Juliénas	$3–$5

RECOMMENDED MÂCONNAIS WINES

White

Mâcon Blanc	$2–$4
St.-Véran	$3–$5
Pouilly-Vinzelles	$3–$5

CHABLIS

The small district of Chablis lies to the northwest of Burgundy proper. The unique character of the wine has eluded numerous imitators around the world, for none can match its steely elegance. The hardiness of the Pinot Chardonnay grape in this sometimes inhospitable climate accounts for much of the great strength and distinction of Chablis. The best wines, *Grand Cru* Chablis, are crisp, dry as flint, almost breathtaking. They have great depth and breed, combined with gentle fruit and a delicate bouquet. Even their color, green-gold, adds to the effect of mossy coolness so appealing on a warm day. Since the *Grand Cru* wines account for only 5 percent of the total production, they are understandably expensive. The second-rank wines, called *Premiers Crus,* are a bit less fine, though still remarkable. Wines with only the *Appellation* Chablis rarely approach the two top ranks in complexity and balance. Petit Chablis, a wine from the outskirts of the region, seems pleasant enough when drunk young but is a thin wine of no distinction in off years. Three Chablis growers whose wines are always of top quality are Fiore, Moreau, and Ropiteau.

RECOMMENDED CHABLIS WINES

White

Chablis	$3–$5
Premiers Crus:	
Montée de Tonnerre, Mont de Milieu, Vaulorent, Fourchaume, Côte de Lechet, Beugnons, Butteaux, Les Forêts, Montmains	$4–$7
Grands Crus:	
Vaudésir, Les Clos, Grenouilles, Valmur, Blanchots, Les Preuses, Bougros	$5–$9

Market day in the old city of Beaune, "the capital of Burgundian wines." Cellars beneath the streets store the district's wines, while above ground the foods of the countryside are offered for sale

THE RHONE VALLEY

The Rhône Valley vineyards that the French call the Côtes du Rhône begin just below Lyons, about thirty miles from the southern end of Beaujolais. Even along the upper stretches of the Côtes du Rhône, the climate is too hot and dry for growing the grape varieties that give the fine wines of Bordeaux, Burgundy, and Champagne. Instead, such strains as the Syrah and Grenache are planted. Although these wines are considered inferior to many others, several of them are of the highest quality. Among the best growers and shippers are Chapoutier, Paul Jaboulet Aîné, Henri Gachet, Baron LeRoy, Doctor Dufays Mousset, Wildman, Brune et Blonde, and Montredon.

RECOMMENDED RHÔNE VALLEY WINES

Red		*White*	
Côtes du Rhône	$2–$3	Condrieu	$10–$20
Cornas	$3–$5	Château Grillet	$10–$20
St. Joseph	$3–$5	Hermitage Blanc	$4–$7
Gigondas	$3–$5		
Côte Rôtie	$4–$7		
Hermitage Rouge	$4–$8	*Rosé*	
Châteauneuf-du-Pape	$5–$10	Tavel	$3–$5
Lirac Rouge	$2–$4	Lirac Rosé	$2–$4

The distinctive pink color of vin rosé is achieved by drawing the wine off the red grape skins after two or three days, before the color deepens

Facing: A robust red wine from the Côtes du Rhône is a good accompaniment to barbecued meats

THE LOIRE VALLEY

The vineyards of the Loire Valley are strung along one of the prettiest rivers in France. Generous quantities of wine, mostly white and rosé, are made all along its vine-clad banks. However, much of the wine is too low in alcohol (under 11 percent) to withstand the rigors of travel. To sample the complete variety of Loire wines, the wine lover must journey to the delightful vineyards in the valley itself. There it is soon discovered that the wines are the most pleasant and engaging *vins du pays* in all France, especially when they are enjoyed in one of the many fine local restaurants, accompanied by some of the light *spécialités de la campagne* and pungent cheese. One town, Sancerre, is as famous for its goat cheese (*chèvre*) as for its wine. Little spheres, pyramids, and cylinders of the chalk-white cheese are sold in markets and restaurants everywhere along the Loire. Though cheese is traditionally served with a full-bodied red wine, the *chèvres* of the Loire seem a perfect complement to the valley's many white wines.

Some of the better growers and shippers are Wildman, Lichine, Ackerman-Laurence, Caves St. Pierre, Gaudry, Château Briacé, Château du Nozet (La Doucette), Château de Montcontour, Monmousseau, and Baumard.

RECOMMENDED LOIRE VALLEY WINES

White

Sancerre	$3–$5
Pouilly-Fumé	$4–$7
Vouvray	$3–$5
Saumur	$3–$4
Savennières	$3–$4
Quarts de Chaumes	$4–$6
Bonnezeaux	$4–$6
Côteaux du Layon	$4–$6
Gros Plant du Pays Nantais	$2–$4
Muscadet	$3–$4
Muscadet-sur-Lie	$3–$5

Red

Saumur-Champigny	$3–$4
Chinon	$3–$5
Bourgueil	$3–$5

Rosé

Anjou Rosé de Cabernet	$3–$5

Facing: The wine man's rule "Buy on water, sell on cheese" is based on the fact that wine tastes better with a good cheese. Apples, too, enhance a wine, and the combination adds up to an enjoyable repast

ALSACE

Not surprisingly, the wines of Alsace are similar to those from the nearby Rhine and Moselle vineyards of Germany. The grape varieties are the same: Riesling, Sylvaner, and Traminer grow in the best plots on both sides of the Rhine. Alsatian wines, however, do not show the German tendency toward sweetness; they are strong, dry, and clean, higher in alcohol and fuller-bodied. The control of Alsatian wines is exercised by a regional organization independent of the French government; it determines which wines are permitted to use the *Appellation d'Origine Contrôlée Vins d'Alsace*, and which grape varieties may be used in their production. Alsatian wines are identified by the names of the grapes from which they are made. As in Germany, the Riesling is the foremost variety. Alsatian Rieslings are dry and full of fruit, with only a trace of sweetness. Somewhat lighter and less elegant is the Sylvaner. Fresh and attractive, Alsatian Sylvaner is the wine to serve when warm weather begins. The Traminer grape gives the richest, fruitiest, most dramatic wines of Alsace. The best are called Gewürztraminer. The German word *gewürz* means "spicy," and indeed the wine is spicy and flavorful, with a concentrated bouquet.

A few other grape varieties are used in Alsace for white wines, and the Pinot Noir yields a pleasant rosé. The Muscat grape, grown the world over for sweet wines, in Alsace gives a crisp, dry, and fruity wine.

Alsatian wines often represent superior values—excellent quality at a reasonable price—because of the tremendous quantities produced, usually more than 10 million cases annually. Most of the wines of Alsace found abroad are exported by large shippers who buy grapes and vinify the grapes themselves. Some of the first-rate firms are Hügel, Trimbach, Jules Muller, Beyer, Preiss-Henny, and Dopff.

RECOMMENDED ALSATIAN WINES

Sylvaner	$3–$5
Riesling	$3–$5
Gewürztraminer	$4–$6

Alsatian wines are known by grape variety rather than place of origin. The Gewürztraminer grape makes the spicy white wine of the region

Facing: A 90-mile Wine Road meanders through the vine-clad hills of Alsace

CHAMPAGNE

Vintners in the United States, Chile, Russia, and countless other countries make a sparkling wine they call "champagne." But strictly speaking, Champagne is the name of a region lying about a hundred miles east and north of Paris—and, more important for our purposes, the name of the wine produced there.

No compromise with quality is permitted in the production of champagne. Only three grape varieties may go into the wine. They are the Pinot Noir, the great red-wine grape of Burgundy; the Pinot Chardonnay, responsible for the finest white Burgundies; and the Pinot Meunier, a black grape, used to a lesser extent. If the Pinot Chardonnay is used exclusively, the grower may call his wine *blanc de blancs*, a phrase which simply means a white wine made from white grapes. *Blanc de blancs* champagne is particularly light and delicate.

Like Bordeaux and Burgundy, Champagne is composed of different districts, each with its own characteristics. The slopes of the large Montagne de Reims section are planted exclusively in Pinot Noir. The grapes from this area yield wines of firmness and great fragrance, with enough acidity to encourage long life. Another district, the Vallée de la Marne, is also planted solely in Pinot Noir. It produces wines that are rounder and richer in flavor than those from the Montagne de Reims. The last but not the least important winegrowing area is the Côtes des Blancs, planted, appropriately enough, in the light-colored Pinot Chardonnay, which contributes notable finesse to the finished wine.

Within these three districts are the various villages that have been officially rated according to the quality of the wines they produce. The most famous communes are Verzenay, Mailly, Bouzy, Ambonnay, Ay, Avize, and Cramant. These towns hold the top, or 100 percent, rating, and the greatest of vintage champagnes contain a high proportion of the superior wine from these villages.

At the yearly Champagne festival an old winepress is operated by people in costumes of earlier times. The harvest baskets, brimming with dark Pinot Noir grapes, have been used in the Champagne region for generations

The Champagne vineyards are the northernmost of all French wine regions. In years when the climate is relatively warm and mild, fine vintage wine can be made. In less favorable years Champagne houses blend the production of great years, average years, and poorer years into a nonvintage wine. To assure that nonvintage champagne retains its standing as a superb wine, no grower is permitted to sell more than 80 percent of his grapes of a successful year for the production of vintage wine. The other 20 percent is used to improve the quality of nonvintage champagne.

Since most champagne is a nonvintage blend, the consumer must rely on the integrity of the various firms. The brand or name of the champagne house is therefore more significant than the vineyard or district. The world-renowned champagne firms have become synonymous with excellence and reliability.

Sparkling wines are produced in regions of France other than Champagne. These are called simply *vins mousseux*, from the French word for effervescent, and they are not entitled to be called champagne. Some of them can be quite good, and they are always less costly than true champagne. The dry sparkling wine from the Haute-Savoie and the fruity *mousseux* of the Loire Valley can be delightful, as can some of the better examples from both Burgundy and Bordeaux. In the eastern part of the Rhône Valley very attractive sparkling wine is produced in considerable quantity.

RECOMMENDED CHAMPAGNE WINES

Mumm, Moët & Chandon, Piper Heidsieck,	Nonvintage $9–$12
Heidsieck Monopole, Charles Heidsieck, Lanson,	
Ayala, Veuve-Cliquot, Krug, Pommery and Greno,	Vintage $11–$15
Deutz and Geldermann, Dom Ruinart, Louis Roederer,	
Taittinger, Pol Roger, Perrier-Jouet, Bollinger,	
Lanson, Laurent Perrier, Mercier	
Moët & Chandon Dom Perignon, Mumm René Lalou,	
Roederer Cristal, Taittinger Comtes de Champagne,	About $25
Laurent Perrier Grand Siècle	

Côteaux Champenois—still Champagne

Ch. de Saran	About $10
Bollinger	$4
Charbaut	$4

RECOMMENDED SPARKLING WINES

White

Clairette de Die	$5–$6
Saumur	
Vouvray	
St.-Péray	
Seyssel (Boyer Brut and Le Duc)	
White Burgundy (Kriter)	

A NÉGOCIANT'S SELECTION

Alsatian wines bear the *Appellation Alsace Contrôlée* and the name of the grape from which they are made. The *négociant*'s name is prominent—an indication of his importance in determining the wine's quality.

A BANNER BRUT

French champagne is so famous that its labels need not say *Appellation Contrôlée.* Cordon Rouge is a nonvintage blend of wines from two or more years.

HOW TO READ A FRENCH WINE LABEL

A CHÂTEAU-BOTTLED BORDEAUX

The property name (Haut-Brion), controlled district (Graves), vintage date (1966), and, as a further guarantee, *Mis en bouteilles au château,* plus *Premier Grand Cru Classé* indicate the select first rank of Bordeaux wines.

A GRAND CRU FROM BURGUNDY

Musigny and other renowned vineyards have their own *Appellations. Cuvée Vieilles Vignes* (Selections from Old Vines) and the numbered bottle indicate greatness.

A PREMIER CRU FROM BURGUNDY

The wine bears the village name, Puligny-Montrachet, and that of a *Premier Cru* vineyard, Les Combettes. *Appellation Contrôlée* refers to the village. *Mise au domaine* indicates estate-bottling in Burgundy.

A V.D.Q.S. WINE FROM THE LOIRE

The name combines the grape (Gros Plant) with the area (Nantes). The key words are *Vin Délimité de Qualité Supérieure*, the designation granted regional wines, better than *vins ordinaires* but not as good as *Appellation Contrôlée*.

A BORDEAUX REGIONAL WINE

Don't confuse this with château-bottled claret. *Appellation Bordeaux Contrôlée* means that the wine may come from anywhere in Bordeaux. *Dans nos chais* (in our cellars)—not the same as *au château*—means that this is a blend from several vineyards.

A TOP BEAUJOLAIS

Since this wine was grown, made, and bottled on an estate properly called a château, the label may say *Mise en bouteille au château*. ("Estate-bottled" is the Burgundy designation.) The neckband proclaims the wine's vintage and awards.

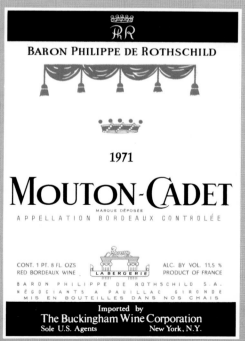

THE COUNTRY WINES OF FRANCE

To enjoy French *vins du pays* we need no longer visit the regions that produce them. Such wines as Cahors, Corbières, Fitou, Bergerac, and Crépy now appear here with increasing frequency. Frenchmen have always appreciated these so-called "little" wines. Most are of V.D.Q.S. status, but in recent years a number of the better ones have been granted the *Appellation Contrôlée* in recognition of their improved quality.

RECOMMENDED COUNTRY WINES OF FRANCE

Red

Cahors	$3–$5
Corbières	$2–$4
Fitou	$2–$4
Minervois	$2–$4
Bandol	$4–$6
Bellet	$2–$5
Côtes de Provence	$2–$3
Bergerac	$2–$4

White

Cassis	$3–$5
Arbois	$4–$7
Château Chalon	$5–$10
Crépy	$3–$5
Étoile	$3–$5
Monbazillac	$2–$4
Montravel	$2–$4
Jurançon	$3–$5
Bandol Blanc de Blancs	$3–$5

Rosé

Bandol	$3–$4
Cassis	$2–$4

OTHER
WINES
OF
THE
WORLD

THE WINES OF GERMANY

I f it is true that adversity builds character in wines as well as in people, nowhere on earth does adversity play a larger part than in molding the magnificent breed of the white wines in Germany. Her greatest vineyards, being among the northernmost on the globe, subject their grapevines to a harrowing succession of physical hardships—cold winters, spring frosts, sunless summers.

What the capricious climate almost seems to strive to prevent—and what the concerned winemaker seeks—is the delicate balance of sugar and acid in the wine that makes the best of it both dulcet and fresh. With acidity alone, the wine snaps sharp and bitter on the tongue; with sweetness alone, the wine lies flat and listless. The golden harmony is struck somewhere in between. And since German wines are relatively low in alcohol (8.5 to 12 percent) the balance of the other constituents becomes even more crucial.

One vine, the Riesling, must be accorded the honor of giving us the finest of German wines. Though its grapes are small and not very juicy, the wines they yield are some of the most wonderful in the world. Also common is the Sylvaner, which is known, too, in Alsace and parts of California. Its wine is less rich and flavorful than the Riesling's. A bottle of average-quality German wine with no grape name on its label is sure to contain wine made mostly from the Sylvaner or from the Müller-Thurgau, a cross of the Riesling and the Sylvaner, planted in many vineyards of the Rheinhessen and the Palatinate. Müller-Thurgau vines are early-ripening, and their wine shows little of the brilliance of the Riesling parent.

In late November or December overripe grapes sometimes freeze on the vine. Picked early in the morning and crushed immediately, they make a sweet rich wine, the rare Eiswein, one of nature's accidents turned to good advantage

Facing: A village on the Rhine, with vineyards climbing the hill behind it, is typical of one of the world's great wine-producing areas

The Gewürztraminer, like the Sylvaner, is widely known abroad for the fresh and intriguing wine it gives in Alsace.

The German wine law of 1971 defines much of the present wine terminology. The German vineyards are officially divided into eleven districts: Ahr, Mittelrhein, Mosel-Saar-Ruwer, Rheingau, Hessiche Bergstrasse, Nahe, Rheinhessen, Rheinpfalz, Franken, Württemberg, and Baden. All produce both mediocre and good wines, but only selected sections of the Rheingau, Mosel-Saar-Ruwer, Nahe, Rheinhessen, and Rheinpfalz regions grow that special 5 percent of Germany's wines prized by connoisseurs.

The 1971 wine law not only named the large winegrowing regions but also defined their various subdivisions. Each of the eleven major wine regions is called a *Gebiet*. In descending order of size, the subdivisions are: the *Bereich* (district), the *Grosslage* (group of vineyards), and the *Einzellage* (small single site). It is the *Einzellagen* that produce the fabulous wines and have the famous names. In general, the more limited the area of a wine's origin, the better the wine.

The wine law of 1971 laid down three basic levels of quality for German wines. *Tafelwein* is the ordinary, everyday beverage making up most of the production. *Qualitäts-wein* (Quality Wine) is the next grade. It must come from recognized grape varieties, be grown in one of the eleven official regions, and have, before fermentation, a minimum level of natural sugar. The third category, *Qualitätswein mit Prädikat* (Quality Wine with Special Attributes), represents the top wines; to these no sugar can be added, and thus they can be produced only in years when nature yields up fully ripened grapes.

The "Special Attributes" are indicated by five German terms, the most general of which is *Kabinett* (spelled only thus); it denotes the lightest and driest of the top-quality wines. *Spätlese* is the next higher distinction. The word means "late picking"; a wine so labeled is made from grapes left on the vine until ripened. A *Spätlese* wine is sweeter and richer than a *Kabinett*. The third designation, *Auslese*, means "select picking": the vintner picks over his grapes and selects only the perfect and fully ripe bunches. In very successful vintages, *Ausleses* are made from grapes on which the "noble rot" (*Botrytis cinerea*; in German, *Edelfäule*) has appeared. Such a wine is sweeter and more interesting still, and proportionately more expensive. *Beerenauslese* is a step up from *Auslese*. Only overripe grapes are picked, singly, to go into one of the very sweet and complex wines labeled *Beerenauslese*, which are not unlike fine French Sauternes.

The fifth designation—*Trockenbeerenauslese*—appears only on wines from great vintages, when the grapes matured well and the *Edelfäule* descended upon them. *Trocken-beerenauslese* wine is made from grapes so ripe that they resemble raisins or dry berries—*Trockenbeeren*. Each of these single fruits must be separated from its less lucky brothers, hence the name, which means "dry berry select picking." These wines are rare and are priced accordingly.

The most important vineyards in Germany's five major wine regions are listed on pages 120–21. In addition, for each region we have listed a few recommendations of our personal favorites. Along with the name of the village and vineyard, we have specified the particular proprietor or estate that has earned a high reputation for each wine. A handful of the selections—Schloss Vollrads and Scharzhofberger for example—are actual estate wines known by the property name rather than by town and vineyard plot.

In good vintages these producers may well make a complete range of wines with the same vineyard name—from the more modest *Qualitätswein* to majestic *Trockenbeerenauslese*. Our price levels are for *Kabinett* wines, with the exact price depending mostly on the quality of the vintage (see the vintage chart, page 155). *Kabinett* wines are more generally available in the United States than those with higher "Special Attributes."

THE RHEINGAU

One of the greatest white-wine regions of the world is on the slopes of the Taunus Mountains, a low range above the Rhine in central Germany, north and east of Mainz. Assmannshausen and Lorch on the west and Hochheim on the east mark the limits of the district, the greatest wines growing in the central section, from Rüdesheim to Eltville.

RECOMMENDED RHEINGAU WINES

Schloss Vollrads Blue-Gold Kabinett	$4–$8
Schloss Johannisberg Orange Seal Kabinett	$4–$8
Hattenheimer Nussbrunnen Kabinett, von Simmern	$4–$7
Rauenthaler Baiken Kabinett, Graf Eltz	$4–$7
Erbacher Marcobrunn Kabinett, von Simmern	$4–$7
Steinberger Kabinett State Domaine	$4–$7
Rüdesheimer Berg Schlossberg Kabinett, von Schorlemer	$3–$6

MOSEL-SAAR-RUWER

The fine Mosel-Saar-Ruwer wines, like most other German wines, are named for the town and vineyard from which they come. The Moselle passes these good vineyards as it flows nearly due north, making its way to Piesport and the first great Moselle wines. Behind the quaint town are the great vineyards—Goldtröpfchen, Falkenberg, Treppchen, and Günterslay. The secret of all the finest Moselles is the interaction of the aristocratic Riesling with the gray slaty soil that covers the steep hills. In Piesport the result is a wine even more delicate than some of the other fine Moselles, one with remarkable fragrance and class.

Amid the rows of Riesling vines that tower like a wall above Bernkastel is the Doktor vineyard, perhaps the most renowned in Germany. Besides Doktor (the wine was once credited with healing properties), Bernkastel boasts the Lay, Graben, Bratenhöfchen, and Schlossberg vineyards, which continue along the great wall of vines as it curves north of the village and crosses the boundary into Graach. Here the best wines are Himmelreich and Domprobst.

The miraculous vertical vineyards continue on to the best plots in the towns of Wehlen and Zeltingen. The preoccupation with sunshine has led to the prevalence of sundials (*Sonnenuhren*) along the river, and certainly the best-known of these is the one that gives its name to the great wine of Wehlen. Indeed nowadays many experts agree that Wehlener Sonnenuhr is a better wine than the famous Doktor. At Zeltingen, as the Moselle reaches a long turn, the wall lowers, but not before producing some exceptionally fine and full-bodied wines.

The Saars and Ruwers triumph in the hottest years, when the wines wrap their steeliness and strength in a clover-honey cloak. Wiltingen is the best-known town in the Saar, with the best-known vineyard, the Scharzhofberg. Among the other vineyards in Wiltingen the better ones are Gottesfuss, Braune Kupp, and Klosterberg. Farther upstream sits the pretty village called Ockfen, where the famous Bockstein vineyard spreads back into the valley behind the few scattered houses. The wine is so light that one can only wonder how it can offer such a range of complex and elegant tastes.

The third valley growing Mosel-Saar-Ruwer wines is that of the Ruwer. The town of Kasel makes pleasant, very pale wines that represent the average. Eitelsbach and Mertesdorf are better known because each is the home of a truly fine estate where great wine is grown. The quality of each wine is very high, the suave blend of floweriness and metallic austerity that is the incredible accomplishment of the best wines from the Mosel-Saar-Ruwer *Gebiet*.

RECOMMENDED MOSEL-SAAR-RUWER WINES

Bernkasteler Schlossberg Kabinett, Wwe. Dr. Thanisch	$4–$8
Graacher Himmelreich Kabinett, J. J. Prüm	$3–$7
Maximin Grünhäuser Herrenberg Kabinett, Schubert	$5–$9
Scharzhofberger Kabinett, Egon Müller	$5–$9
Josephshofer Kabinett, von Kesselstatt	$4–$8
Piesporter Goldtröpfchen Kabinett, Viet	$3–$7
Ürziger Würzgarten, Kabinett, Jos. Beeres	$3–$7

THE RHEINHESSEN

The Rheinhessen, or Hesse, as it is often known in English, is a vast rectangle of rolling, fertile farmland whose vineyards grow quantities of soft, light wines—except on one small section of the eastern slopes, which falls away toward the Rhine and produces some of the finest wine in Germany. The great vineyards, planted partly in the Riesling grape, rise up from the "Rheinfront" as the river flows by in a crescent from Oppenheim to Nackenheim. Between these two towns stands Nierstein, home of the finest of all Rheinhessen wines, considered by the Germans themselves to be the country's most famous wine town.

In a plentiful year, more than half a million gallons of wine may earn the right to the name Niersteiner, surely the Rhine's most general village name, as Bernkastel is along the Moselle. To obtain a topflight Niersteiner, it is important therefore to make sure that the name of a specific vineyard also appears on the bottle. When the plot named on the label is a good one and the vine is the Riesling (or even in a few special cases the Sylvaner), the wine will be noble indeed, with much fruit and finesse. The greatest names are Hipping, Rehbach, Orbel, Rosenberg, and Glock, but Kranzberg, Pettenthal, Zehnmorgen, and Oelberg also give remarkably good wine in a successful vintage.

RECOMMENDED RHEINHESSEN WINES

Niersteiner Hipping Kabinett, Karl L. Schmitt	$4–$7
Niersteiner Orbel Kabinett, Franz K. Schmitt	$4–$7
Oppenheimer Sackträger Kabinett, Senfter	$4–$7

THE RHEINPFALZ (THE PALATINATE)

The Rheinpfalz is Germany's largest winegrowing region, vines being planted from the border with northern Alsace to Worms. In a plentiful year nearly 40,000 acres under vine yield almost 20 million gallons of wine. Most of the wine is harsh, with a distinct taste of the soil, passable only if quaffed icy cold on the flower-decked terrace of an old inn at one of the many charming towns that grace the countryside.

Wine of top quality is produced only in one tiny section west of Speyer and Mannheim: a serene trail of vineyards called the Mittelhaardt, running north to Dackenheim from Neustadt. And one patch of the Mittelhaardt grows wines that outclass any others from the district. The core of the Mittelhaardt—from Ruppertsberg to Kallstadt—produces white wines that are among the best in Germany. Less than a mile from Ruppertsberg is Deidesheim, where many of the vineyards are owned by the three great wine men of Pfalz (known as "the three Bs"): Bassermann-Jordan, von Buhl, Bürklin-Wolf. In no other section of German vineyards is there a comparable trio making most of the great wine. The best Deidesheimers are invariably Riesling.

RECOMMENDED RHEINPFALZ WINES

Forster Jesuitengarten Kabinett, Bassermann-Jordan	$4–$7
Forster Kirchenstück Kabinett, von Buhl	$4–$7
Deidesheimer Herrgottsacker Kabinett, Winzerverein Deidesheim	$3–$6

THE GREAT GERMAN WHITE-WINE VINEYARDS

Before the wine law of 1971 became effective, the various German winegrowing districts counted more than 30,000 individually named vineyards. The law has grouped many of the smaller plots together, reducing the total number of vineyard names to about 3,000. Of this still large number, a relatively few consistently produce the finest German white wines—these are the 140-odd vineyards listed below, arranged by region and town. The top vineyards are rated *great* (incomparable, like the First Growths of Bordeaux or the *Grands Crus* of Burgundy), *very good* (always regal, elegant, with finesse and breed), *good* (still remarkable, far above average).

Town	Vineyard	Rating	Town	Vineyard	Rating
The Great Vineyards of the Rheingau			Neumagen	Rosengärchten	good
				Laudamusberg	good
Rüdesheim	Berg Roseneck	very good	Piesport	Goldtröpfchen	very good
	Berg Rottland	very good		Gunterslay	good
	Berg Schlossberg	very good		Treppchen	good
	Bischofsberg	good		Falkenberg	good
	Klosterberg	good			
			Wintrich	Grosserherrgott	good
Geisenheim	Klaus	very good		Ohligsberg	very good
	Kilzberg	good			
			Brauneberg	Hasenläufer	very good
Johannisberg	Schloss Johannisberg	great		Juffer	very good
	Vogelsang	very good		Juffer-Sonnenuhr	good
	Hölle	very good			
	Klaus	very good	Bernkastel	Doktor	great
				Graben	great
Winkel	Schloss Vollrads	great		Lay	very good
	Hasensprung	very good		Bratenhöfchen	very good
	Jesuitengarten	good		Schlossberg	very good
				Rosenberg	good
Hallgarten	Schönhell	very good			
	Hendelberg	good	Graach	Himmelreich	very good
	Jungfer	good		Domprobst	good
Oestrich	Lenchen	good	Wehlen	Sonnenuhr	great
	Doosberg	good		Nonnenberg	good
				Klosterberg	good
Hattenheim	Steinberg	great			
	Mannberg	very good	Zeltingen	Sonnenuhr	very good
	Wisselbrunnen	very good		Schlossberg	very good
	Nussbrunnen	very good		Himmelreich	very good
	Schützenhaus	good			
			Urzig	Würzgarten	very good
Erbach	Markobrunn	great			
	Siegelsberg	very good	Erden	Treiichen	very good
	Steinmorgen	good		Prälat	good
Rauenthal	Baiken	great			
	Gehrn	great			
	Langenstück	very good	**SAAR**		
	Rothenberg	good			
			Wawern	Goldberg	good
Hochheim	Kirchenstück	good		Herrenberg	good
	Domdechaney	good			
	Stein	good	Kanzem	Sonnenberg	good
	Hölle	good		Altenberg	good
			Wiltingen	Scharzhofberg	great
				Gottesfuss	very good
The Great Vineyards of Mosel-Saar-Ruwer				Klosterberg	good
				Braune Kupp	good
MOSEL					
Trittenheim	Apotheke	very good	Ayl	Herrenberger	very good
	Altärchen	good	Ockfen	Bockstein	great

Town	Vineyard	Rating
	Herrenberg	very good
	Geisberg	good
Oberemmel	Hütte	good

RUWER

Town	Vineyard	Rating
Mertesdorf	Maximin Grünhaus	great
Eitelsbach	Karthäuserhofberg	great
Kasel	Neis'chen	very good
	Hitzlay	good
Avelsbach	Herrenberg	good
	Altenberg	good
	Hammerstein	good

The Great Vineyards of the Rheinhessen

Town	Vineyard	Rating
Oppenheim	Sackträger	very good
	Kreuz	good
	Schlossberg	good
Nierstein	Orbel	great
	Hipping	great
	Ölberg	great
	Glock	very good
	Rehbach	very good
	Zehnmorgen	very good
	Kranzberg	very good
	Rosenberg	good
Nackenheim	Rothenberg	very good
	Engelsberg	good
Bodenheim	Hoch	good
	Burgweg	good
Bingen	Scharlachberg	very good
	Rosengarten	good
	Kapellenberg	good

The Great Vineyards of the Nahe

Town	Vineyard	Rating
Bad Kreuznach	Narrenkappe	very good
	Brückes	very good
	Kronenberg	good
Norheim	Kafels	good
	Dellchen	good

Town	Vineyard	Rating
Roxheim	Birkenberg	good
	Höllenpfad	good
Niederhausen	Hermannshöhle	great
	Rosenheck	very good
	Klamm	good
Schloss Böckelheim	Kupfergrube	great
	Felsenberg	very good
	Königsberg	very good
	Mühlberg	good

The Great Vineyards of the Rheinpfalz (The Palatinate)

Town	Vineyard	Rating
Königsbach	Idig	very good
	Reiterpfad	good
Ruppertsberg	Gaisböhl	very good
	Spiess	good
	Hoheburg	good
Deidesheim	Herrgottsacker	great
	Grainhübel	great
	Kieselberg	very good
	Leinhöhle	very good
	Hohenmorgen	very good
	Kalkhofen	good
	Mäushöhle	good
Forst	Kirchenstück	great
	Jesuitengarten	great
	Freundstück	very good
	Ungeheuer	very good
	Pechstein	good
	Elster	good
Wachenheim	Gerümpel	great
	Rechbächel	very good
	Böhlig	good
	Goldbächel	good
Bad Dürkheim	Hochbenn	very good
	Michelsberg	good
	Fuchsmantel	good
Ungstein	Herrenberg	good
	Michelsberg	good
Kallstadt	Horn	good
	Kronenberg	good
	Steinacker	good

A REGIONAL MOSELLE

Bernkastel is now also the appellation for the middle section of vineyards *(Bereich)* in the Mosel-Saar-Ruwer. To avoid confusion with the famous town, wines from this section must be labeled "Bereich Bernkastel." *Qualitätswein* is the legal designation for second-rank wines.

A TYPICAL TOPFLIGHT MOSELLE

The suffix "-er" indicates that the wine comes from the town, not the *Bereich*. V.D.P.V. *Verband Deutscher Prädikatwein Versteigerer* means that this wine was made by a member of an association of top-quality wine producers.

HOW TO READ A GERMAN WINE LABEL

A NEW RHEINGAU REGIONAL

Erntebringer is the section *(Grosslage)* that includes Geisenheim and Johannisberg. "Johannisberger" tells us that the wine was grown in the vineyards associated with that town.

A GREAT RHEINGAU ESTATE WINE

Schloss Johannisberg is the home of many great Rheingau wines. *Grunlack* ("green label") is always used for Schloss Johannisberg *Spätlese* wines. *Erzeuger-Abfullung* indicates château *(Schloss)*-bottled wine.

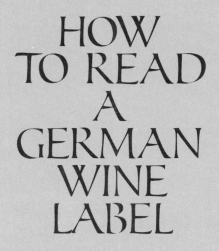

THE NAHE

The town of Bingen in the Rheinhessen stands at the mouth of the river Nahe where it meets the Rhine. In this lower part of the Nahe Valley, the wines often resemble those of the Rheingau, without achieving the level of excellence common to the great growths of Germany's most famous vineyard land.

Upstream from Bingen lie the vineyards that give the best Nahe wines. These begin just below Bad Kreuznach—an old spa that is the center of the Nahewein trade—where the best sites are Narrenkappe and Brückes. Above Kreuznach, vines cling to a narrow path at the base of the Rotenfels. They make a spicy, profound wine called Rotenfelser Bastei.

Niederhausen and Schloss Böckelheim, the next two towns up the river, have the greatest vineyards of the valley, Hermannshöhle and Kupfergrube. Here the wines resemble some of the good Saars and Ruwers. Both of the fine plots are on the Kupferberg ("copper mountain") midway between the two towns.

Next to the Kupfergrube are the admirable cellars of the State Domain in Hesse, where some of the best white wine in all Germany comes to life. The well-known Schloss Böckelheim name has long been given to all the regional wine made in this part of the Nahe. One can be sure that the wine in question is a fine one from the town itself if the label also includes a specific vineyard name, such as Kupfergrube, Königsfels, Felsenberg, Heimberg, In den Felsen.

RECOMMENDED WINE

White
Schloss Böckelheimer Kupfergrube Kabinett   about $5

A venerable cellar master thoughtfully judges his wine's bouquet. Smell is as important as taste in evaluating a wine

Facing: *Autumn Landscape: Vintaging* (portion) by Lucas van Valckenborch, Flemish, 1585

GERMAN WINE REGIONS

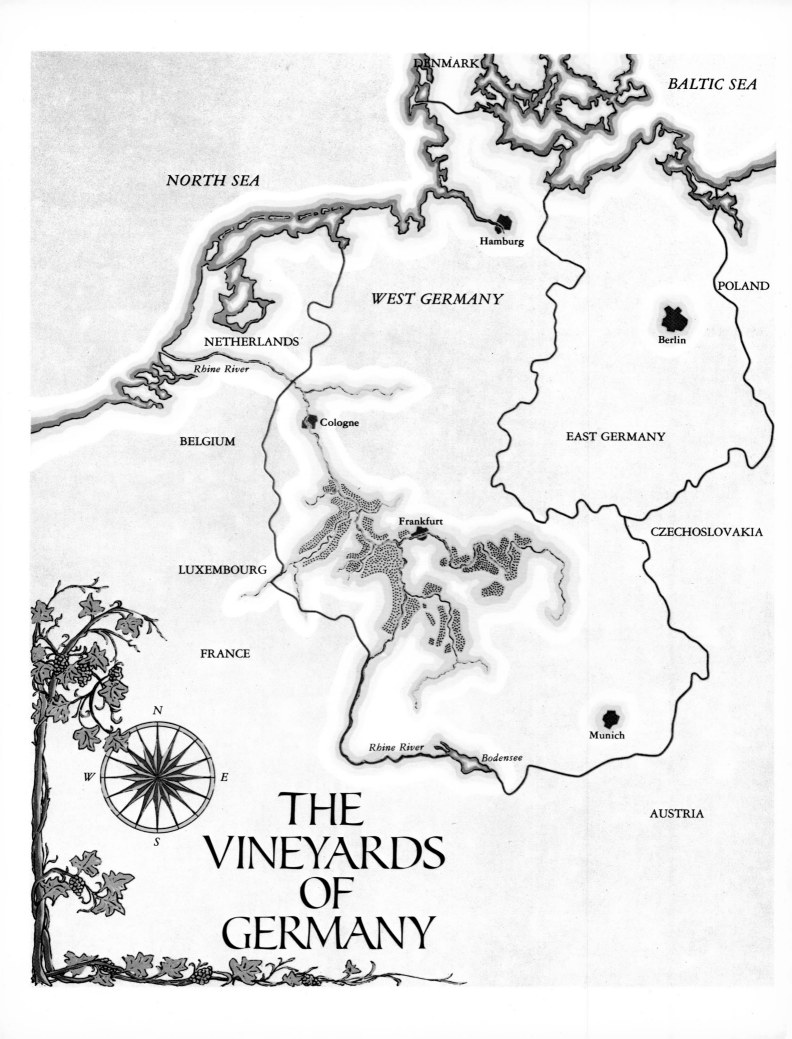

BALTIC SEA

DENMARK

NORTH SEA

POLAND

WEST GERMANY

Hamburg

NETHERLANDS

Rhine River

Berlin

BELGIUM

Cologne

EAST GERMANY

CZECHOSLOVAKIA

Frankfurt

LUXEMBOURG

FRANCE

N

W   E

S

Rhine River

Bodensee

Munich

AUSTRIA

THE
VINEYARDS
OF
GERMANY

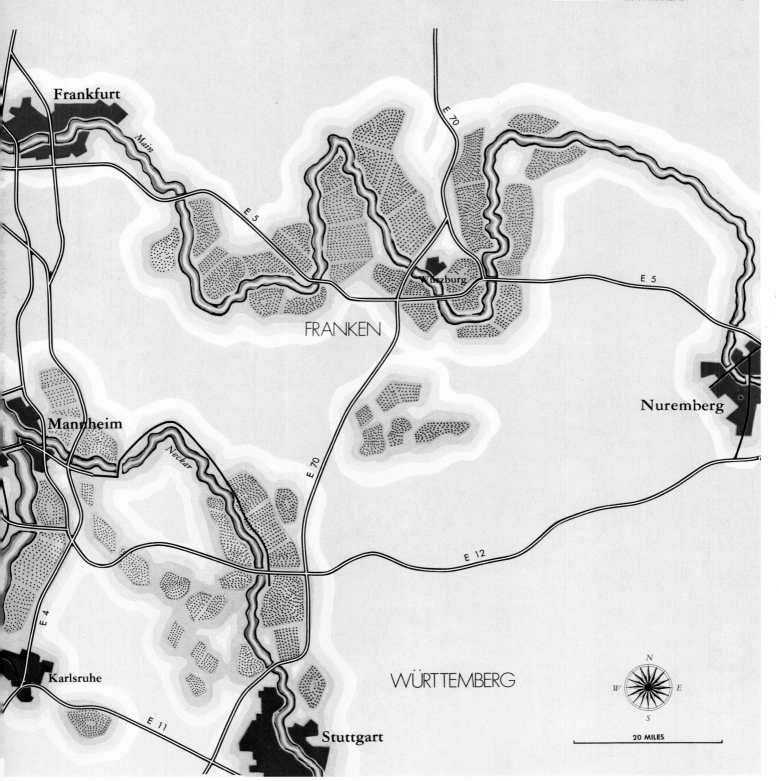

THE WINES OF ITALY

One joy that all Italy shares is wine. If united on no other count, Italians make up the greatest body of winemakers and wine drinkers in the world. Like the nation itself, the wines of Italy are anything but unified. The government has, to be sure, made a grand effort to delimit growing regions and to set standards of quality for the best wines. The laws of 1963 have helped to impose some semblance of order on the vast disarray of Italian wines, and these specifications promise much for the future of Italian wines.

The notable wines of Italy are isolated summits rising from a sea of everyday wines. These relatively outstanding wines are named in several ways. Many good Italian wines (and the better ones, likely to be found abroad, are our primary concern) take the name of the town or region in which they were first produced. Other wine names derive from a grape plus a town or district. Still other names are the product of fantasy or are allusions to historical anecdote. The best wines of Italy are red, and the name of at least one is known around the world—Chianti, which grows on the Tuscan hills south of Florence and north of Siena.

No matter what its name or origin, an Italian wine exported to the United States is likely to carry the words *Denominazione di Origine Controllata* on the label. The phrase, literally "Controlled Denomination of Origin," is usually abbreviated to D.O.C. The concept is a rough equivalent of the French *Appellation Contrôlée*.

The laws are as strict and detailed as those of France, but their enforcement can hardly be called as zealous. As a result, hundreds of wines from everywhere in Italy—deserving and undeserving, great and small—have sought and won the D.O.C. Although still new, and far from perfect, the laws have nevertheless done much to delimit special wine areas, roughly along the lines used in other Common Market countries. This assurance to the consumer of some sort of guide to origin and quality has made a wider variety of Italian wines popular abroad.

Following is a list of Italian wines with their regions, a brief comment, and our rating, and, finally, our recommendations of specific bottles, with their approximate prices.

Ischia, sister island of Capri, produces a light dry white wine, perfect for drinking at its colorful summer festival

ITALIAN TABLE WINES

RED WINES

Wine	District	Comments	Rating
Aglianico	South-central Italy between Bari and Naples	Full, pronounced character, long-lived.	good
Amarone	Veneto, near Verona	Dark, full, complex.	great
Barbaresco	Piedmont, near Alba (south of Turin)	Light, well-balanced, enjoyable.	very good
Barbera	Piedmont, especially east of Turin	Common and inexpensive; named for the Barbera grape.	acceptable
Barbera d'Alba	Piedmont, around Alba	Smooth, flavorful, good value.	good
Barbera d'Asti	Piedmont, around Asti	Excellent; deep character.	very good
Bardolino	Southeastern shore of Lake Garda, near Verona	Very light in color and taste, to be drunk young.	good
Barolo	Southern Piedmont	Fine wine, powerful and subtle.	great
Brunello di Montalcino	Tuscany, south of Siena	Scarce, elegant, rewarding.	great
Chianti	Tuscany	Agreeable, undistinguished, easy to drink.	good
Chianti Classico	Tuscany, between Siena and Florence	Good all-round wine, fruity and dry.	very good
Chianti Riserva	Tuscany, between Siena and Florence	One of the best; finesse and long life.	great
Gattinara	North Piedmont, near Lake Maggiore	Slow to mature, rich and complex.	great
Ghemme	North Piedmont, near Lake Maggiore	Long-lived, soft, very pleasant.	very good
Gragnano	South of Naples, near Sorrento	Almost a Beaujolais; fruity, sweetish.	good
Grignolino	Piedmont	Attractive and pleasant; grape does well in California.	good
Grumello	East of Lake Como, near Swiss border	Sturdy; dry, deep crimson.	very good
Inferno	East of Lake Como, near Swiss border	Rich, full-bodied, austere.	very good
Lago di Caldaro	Near Bolzano in Tyrol	Fragrant, light, fresh.	good
Lambrusco	Near Bologna	Slightly sparkling, fruity, sweetish.	acceptable
Nebbiolo d'Alba	Piedmont, around Alba	Agreeable, like a lighter Barolo.	good
Santa Maddalena	North of Bolzano in Tyrol	Clean, charming, tart.	good
Sassella	East of Lake Como, near Swiss border	Firm, deep-colored; ages well.	very good

Wine	District	Comments	Rating
Spanna	North Piedmont, near Lake Maggiore	Closely related to Gattinara and sometimes even better; grown just outside the delimited zone for Gattinara.	great
Torgiano	Central Italy, near Perugia	Robust, rich, full.	good
Valgella	East of Lake Como, near Swiss border	Lighter than some of its neighbors.	very good
Valpolicella	Just north of Verona	Quality varies; best are velvety and light.	good

INDICE DI TVTTI LI VINI CHE SI TROVANO IN ROMA.

Maluagia
Guarnaccia
Moscatello
Greco di Soma
Greco di Pusilico
Greco di Rasina
Greco della torre
Greco d'Ischia
Pusilico rosso
Chiarello
Centola
Lagrima
Calabrese
Coda cauallo rosso
Vino San Giouanni
Asprino
San Seuerino
Mazzacane
Veenotico
Vino di Santa Rosella
Corso di taglia moscato
Corso di pietra nera
Corso d. Brand.
Latino
Beluedere
Granatino d. Spagna
Vino di Vico
Vino di sette terze
Corso
Pietra nera
Vino Salernitano

Mangiaguerra
Scalea
Vino Francese
Trebiano
Aglianito
Vino d. Paula
Romania
Vino d. Risotollo
Porto Hercole
Vino d. Rosolia
Razzese
Albano
Castel Gandolfo
Marini
La Riccia
Frascati
L'anguillara
Vino del monte
Vino de rocca de Papa
Montarano
Carignella
Vino di Talaggio
Terracina
Caprarola
Turpia
Monte di S.ta Maria
Galese
Greco di Castello
Moscatello di Montefiascone
Vino di Montopol

Vino d'Oruieto
Greco di Spoleti
Vino d. Torzett
Vino d'Orte
Vino di Corzezze
Vino de Cauarini
Vino d. monte rotondo
Vino de la Mentana
Vino d. formelle
Vino di Bracciano
Vino di Galeri
Vino d. Genzano
Vino d. Caui
Vino de L'Isola
Vino d. Hotona
Vino d. Sermoneta
Vino d. Montefortino
Vino della Molara
Vino d. Campagnano
Vino Valariano
Vino d. Nezano
Vino d. Gauignano
Sauell
Vino d. Sutry
Vino d. Velletri
Vino Verralla
Romanesco
Vino di monte Pulciano
Vino riuoenato
Raspato

Nicolai van Aelst forma

WHITE WINES

Wine	District	Comments	Rating
Capri	Island in the Bay of Naples	Pale and very dry.	good
Cortese	Piedmont	Agreeable and light.	very good
Est! Est!! Est!!!	At Montefiascone, north of Rome	Common and undistinguished.	acceptable
Etna	On the slopes of the Sicilian volcano	Dry, almost spicy.	good
Frascati	Hills outside Rome	Popular, but little more.	acceptable
Ischia	Island of Ischia, in the Bay of Naples	Refreshing, pale, dry.	good
Lacrima Christi	Mt. Vesuvius, near Naples	Soft, sweetish, golden.	very good
Lugana	Southern shore of Lake Garda	Not well known, but good.	good
Orvieto	Umbria, north of Rome	Sweet version is best.	good
Riesling	Alto Adige	Lighter than its German cousins.	good
Soave	Just east of Verona	Attractive, agreeable, light and dry.	very good

Wine	District	Comments	Rating
Termeno	Tyrol	Fragrant and spicy; Gewürztraminer grape.	good
Valtellina Bianco	East of Lake Como, near Swiss border	Refreshing, light, tart.	good
Verdicchio	Near Adriatic coast in central Italy	Distinctive, very dry.	good
Verdiso	North of Venice	Fine; unusual bouquet and texture.	good

DESSERT AND SPARKLING WINES

Wine	District	Comments	Rating
Marsala	Sicily	One of the great fortified wines of Europe. Some are sweet, some dry.	very good
Cagliari	Sardinia	Strong, sweet dessert wine.	good
Pantelleria	Island off of Sicily	Similar to Cagliari; also made from Muscat grape.	acceptable
Moscato di Siracusa	Syracuse	Resembles sweet natural wines from Mediterranean vineyards.	acceptable
Moscato Canelli	Canelli in the Piedmont near Asti	Pale, sweetish Muscat.	good
Asti Spumanti	Asti	Very sweet, sparkling Moscato.	acceptable
Gran Spumanti or Spumanti Brut	Asti	Made by classic *méthode champenoise* from Pinot-grape wines.	good

RECOMMENDED ITALIAN WINES

Red

Valpolicella, Bertani	about $3
Chianti Classico, Nozzole	about $4
Barolo, Marchese Spinola	about $5
Spanna Campi Raudii, Vallana	about $6
Chianti Riserva Ducale, Ruffino	about $8

White

Orvieto Secco, Ruffino	about $4
Soave, Bolla	about $4
Verdicchio, Fazi-Battaglia	about $4

Dessert and Sparkling Wines

Florio Marsala—dry or sweet	about $4
Asti Spumanti, Cinzano	about $7

A smiling sun and plump grapes carved on a barrelhead of
Ruffino Chianti hint at the delightful wine within

THE WINES OF SPAIN

Sherries are without a doubt the greatest wines of Spain, and the best of them rank with the finest wines of any country in the world. Spain's red Rioja wines can be exceedingly fine, even if they cannot be reckoned among the world's greatest. The bulk of Spain's production, the red *vino corriente,* or common wine, is seldom worthy of being bottled, and is usually sold in carafe. But from Andalusia to Catalonia some good and honest table wines are made that rank with the simple, inexpensive country wines of other European nations.

RIOJA WINES

The finest Spanish table wines grow in a rocky, desolate area along the banks of the river Ebro. The Río Oja, which joins the Ebro, has given its name to the district as a whole.

Rioja is often compared to Bordeaux. Similarities do exist—both wines are deep, tannic, long-lived, and elegant—but the differences are just as great, if not greater. Red Bordeaux ages in wood for two to three years, then in glass bottles until it is ready to drink. By contrast, red Riojas may spend seven, eight, or even a dozen years in wooden barrels before bottling. The Spanish favor aging the wine in wood rather than in glass. As a result, Riojas take on a tawny color and absorb much of the vanilla scent of the oak. Once bottled, Riojas remain more static than Bordeaux wines. They do not soften and develop bouquet to nearly the same extent. Although much of the tannin—the acid that enables red wines to live in the bottle for many years—is lost during the years in barrel, enough remains so that the wine can enjoy a very long life. Riojas of ten, fifteen, or twenty years are common. They are not invariably great wines, but they offer a smooth, fragrant, memorable wine experience. To that extent, they may well be compared to the clarets of Bordeaux.

Los Borrachos (The Drinkers), Diego Velázquez, c. 1629

Facing: At the *Feria* in Jerez each September the new vintage is blessed. Beautiful local girls carry baskets of sherry grapes to a press where husky men tread out the juice

About two dozen wineries, or *bodegas,* make nearly all the district's wine. Some of the important ones are La Rioja Alta, Vinícola del Norte, Bodegas Bilbainas, Roijanas, Federico Paternina, Marqués de Murrieta, and Marqués de Riscal. Most of these and the other major firms own vineyards in which they grow their own grapes, although they also buy grapes from many of the smaller producers.

Wine labels usually bear the brand name or some special distinction added by the bottler to the basic Rioja appellation. A number of the best bottles are wrapped in a light wire mesh. This covering is more than a decoration: to a wine trade that reveres age almost for its own sake, the wire mesh is valuable as a means to prevent tampering with the dates printed on the labels. Riojas are finding a larger, more important, and more demanding audience outside Spain.

RECOMMENDED RIOJA WINES

Red

Marqués de Cáceres	about $4
Marqués de Murrieta	about $5
Marqués de Riscal	about $5

White

René Barbier Blanco	about $3
Marqués de Murrieta Blanco	about $5

SHERRY

The corner of Andalusia that is sherry country lies south of Seville and borders on the Atlantic. At its center is the town that gives the wine its name, Jerez de la Frontera, around which vineyards extend for more than a dozen miles in every direction. In Jerez, as in Champagne, the key to the light, subtle, remarkable wines is white chalk. In the French earth, the chalk crumbles, but in Spain it forms a hard, brilliant crust on top of the ground. The special soils containing high proportions of chalk are called *albarizas.* Without them, sherry would have none of its world-famous finesse; it would be but another of the strong, alcoholic, fortified beverages found all around the Mediterranean. The Palomino is *the* grape of Jerez, accounting for more than 80 percent of all wine grown there. The Palomino grape and the *albariza* soil are crucial for the wine before it reaches the *bodegas,* where nature continues her capricious hold on the sherry through the little-understood action of the yeastlike fungus, or *flor.* But it is in the blending of the *solera* that nature yields to the hand of man.

The *solera* as a whole is a rank of four or five casks perched one on top of another. The uppermost barrel holds the youngest wines. The one below it contains older wine, the next lower one a blend of wine that is older still. In the bottom barrel is the oldest and most mature wine, the wine that will find its way into a shipper's blend. As the cellar master draws off some of this wine from the bottom cask, the butt is refilled with some of the younger wine from the barrel above. This cask likewise is refreshed with sherry from the one above it, and so forth. When the top barrel needs refilling, the replacement wine comes from the "nurseries" of young wines, the *criaderas.* The magic of the *solera* is that it produces a consistent wine.

The *solera* system precludes the classification of sherry wine by vintage years, but dates are sometimes to be seen on fine sherries. Such dates as 1850, 1879, 1906 indicate when the first wine went into the bottom barrel, and sherry bearing a *solera* date should come exclusively from that one series of casks. The *solera* date is a very far cry from the vintage date, but the *solera* date has its own significance: an old *solera* sherry will have more complexity and finesse than any recent blend could ever hope to muster.

Dated solera sherries are the exception rather than the rule in the *bodegas* of Jerez. Most of the production of a sherry firm is wine chosen from several of its stacks of barrels, then blended into one of the many sorts of sherry the firm offers. Among the important houses are Diez Hermanos, Williams & Humbert, Harvey, Pedro Domecq, Wisdom & Warter, Duff Gordon, Gonzalez Byass, Sandeman, Terry, Garvey, Cano, and Rivero. Each of these concerns makes a selection of sherries ranging from very dry to very sweet.

Sherries develop into two main types—Fino and Oloroso. The driest sherries are those called Fino. They are generally considered to be the best and the most elegant. No serious wine expert could complete his list of the great wines of the world without including the Fino of Jerez.

A Fino reared not in Jerez but in Sanlúcar de Barrameda is called a Manzanilla. Though the soils, grapes, and production of the two centers do not differ substantially, a Manzanilla is a Manzanilla and never a Fino *tout pur*. Manzanillas are usually the palest and driest of all sherries, even drier than the Finos from Jerez itself. But though the wine in a bottle labeled "Manzanilla" is almost certain to be dry, sweeter versions of the wine can be found.

Amontillado comes darker, stronger, and richer than either Manzanilla or Fino. When the magical *flor* growing on the surface of the young sherry turns brown, cellar masters know that this wine is destined to become an Amontillado.

The Olorosos are the sherries with the most body and substance. Quite the opposite of the delicate, racy Fino, the Oloroso has a distinct fatness and pungent power that linger long on the palate. Sweetened Olorosos are developed into the dark Amoroso and Cream Sherries. Vintners add very strong, very sweet wine made from the Pedro Ximénez grape to make both Amorosos and Cream Sherries, using an especially dark wine to color the Amoroso.

RECOMMENDED SHERRIES

Domecq La Ina Fino	about $6
Gonzalez Byass Tio Pepe Fino	about $6
Harvey's Bristol Cream	about $8
Rivero Trocadero Amontillado	about $4
Williams & Humbert Dry Sack	about $6

THE WINES OF PORTUGAL

For many generations of English-speaking wine drinkers, Portugal meant port, the incomparable dessert wine grown on the terraced rock slopes of the river Douro in the wild northeast of the country. For many of today's young wine drinkers, Portugal means not only port but two other wines as well: the vastly popular Mateus Rosé and Vinhos Verdes, both light, fresh table wines.

Whether one chooses the noble port or the simple, satisfying table wine, the contents of the bottle are governed by the regulations of the exemplary Portuguese wine laws. The regulations have done a great deal on the local and national level to improve the quality of the wines and to protect their names from misuse. There have been no known cases of false labeling in Portugal.

TABLE WINES

In the northwest corner of the country is the demarcated region for Vinhos Verdes. These "green wines"—green because the grapes are picked young and the wines drunk young—have a slight natural sparkle, owing to the secondary fermentation in the bottle. This characteristic is especially appealing in the white Vinhos Verdes. Hardly refined or great wines, they are not meant for laying down. Their very short life span makes Vinhos Verdes unlikely candidates for massive exportation.

Another wine from northern Portugal, Dão, needs bottle aging and thus is exported in greater quantities than the green wines. While the important Vinhos Verdes are white wines, the Dãos are reds (though white ones can be very good). These red wines are a blend of a number of different grape varieties. They are strong and rather high in alcohol, resembling the Rhône wines of France or some of the bigger Riojas from Spain. With time, red Dãos develop a good bouquet, but with more than ten years of bottle age they tend to fade.

The Douro, famous for port, also produces a popular table wine—Mateus Rosé—at Vila Real

Facing: Narrow sailboats carry casks of new port down the Douro River to the shippers' warehouses near Oporto, where the wines will be blended and aged

RECOMMENDED PORTUGUESE WINES

Red

Grão Vasco Dão	about $3

White

Casal Garcia Vinho Verde	about $3

Rosé

Mateus	about $3
Lancer's	about $4

PORT

There are five basic types of port: Vintage, Crusted, Tawny, Ruby, and White. Vintage Port, the best of them, is made, as the name suggests, from grapes grown in one specific year. The wine is a blend of different wines from different *quintas,* but it is all wine from one year, that indicated on the bottle. Once blended in the fashion of its particular house, the port spends two years in wooden casks. Curiously, many Vintage Ports are bottled not in Portugal but in London, long the most important city outside Portugal in the port wine trade. Once in glass, the vintage wines begin a lengthy period of slow maturation, traditionally twenty years. The wine throws a considerable deposit as it develops. Unlike other wines', port's sediment does not fall to the bottom of the bottle but clings to its sides. This is the veil-like "crust" which must be carefully considered when the wine is to be drunk. Decanting, an absolute necessity, must be deftly carried out to ensure that none of the crust breaks and clouds the wine. Once decanted, the port should be consumed at one sitting. Like any other fine old wine, Vintage Port will not keep after prolonged exposure to the air.

Crusted Port is like Vintage Port—elegant, deep, rich—except that it is a blend of wine from several vintages. Crusted Port, whose name refers to its characteristic sediment, matures in glass bottles, as does Vintage Port. Though its age cannot be exactly calculated, Crusted Port is a very fine wine.

Tawny Port matures in casks, not in bottles. The interaction of wood, wine, and air softens its taste and removes its purple robe. Tawny is lighter than Vintage Port, and it does not need to be handled with so much reverential care.

Ruby Port is common port: forthrightly red, rich, and sweet. Though offering none of the finesse or range of a Vintage, Crusted, or even a Tawny, Ruby Port is a pleasant enough drink at a much lower price.

RECOMMENDED PORT WINES

Cockburn's Special Reserve	about $7
Sandeman's Partners' Port	about $7
Vintage Ports from Hooper, Dow, Graham, Warre, Fonseca, Robertson, Sandeman, Quinta do Noval, Croft, A. J. da Silva, Taylor	$10–$25

MADEIRA

Madeiras come in every type, from dry to sweet, from golden to brown, from light to rich. Today they are known by grape variety; the name of the grape on the bottle tells us what to expect when we pull the cork.

First, there is Sercial. This is a light, dry wine suitable for an aperitif, for the soup course, and, as many Madeira lovers will tell you, for drinking straight through the meal. Dry as it is, the taste is only slightly acid. It is smooth and tender on the tongue, with a refreshing aftertaste. Sercial is the palest in color, a light gold, but the term "pale" is misleading, for it has brightness, or sheen.

Next is Verdelho, not so dry as Sercial, but definitely not sweet. There is a little less tang, a little more softness, and a warm amber color. Verdelho, too, can be the constant companion, the drink with hors d'oeuvres, with soup, with a bit of sweet. This grape is related to the Pedro Ximénez of Spain, but, like the Sercial grape, when grown on the island of Madeira it develops a special quality.

Bual, the third type of Madeira, is a medium-sweet wine with a richer, deeper amber color. It is admired for its delicate balance, its pungent bouquet. It is full-bodied without being overpowering.

Malmsey, the richest Madeira, carries a name that goes back farther than the history of the island. The first Malmsey probably came from the island of Cyprus. It was a sweet, heavy wine much in demand in the fourteenth and fifteenth centuries. When Portuguese settlers arrived on Madeira, they planted the Malvoisie grape, from which Malmsey is made. This has always been a scarce and expensive wine. It is rich and round, with a heady perfume and a deep brown color. Malmsey fans will not drink their wine with a rich dessert; they maintain that the subtleties of the wine are submerged by competing flavors. For them, the only suitable accompaniments are nuts or simple biscuits.

RECOMMENDED MADEIRA WINES

Justino Sercial	$5
Leacock Malmsey	$6
Cossart Gordon Bual	$7

A selection of Madeiras bottled for export to the United States seen against the blue of Funchal Bay

OTHER RECOMMENDED WINES

AUSTRIA
White

Schloss Graffenegg, Prince von Metternich	about $3
Gumpoldskirchner Königswein Count George	about $3

SWITZERLAND
Red

Dôle du Mont	about $7

White

Neuchâtel, Château d'Auvernier	about $6
Fendant les Murettes	about $7
Aigle les Murailles	about $9

HUNGARY
Red

Egri Bikaver	about $4

White

Lake Balaton Riesling	about $3
Tokay Aszu, 5 Puttonyos	about $6

YUGOSLAVIA
Red

Adriatica Cabernet Istria	about $3
Slovin Cabernet	about $3

White

Slovin Jerusalem Traminec	about $3

RUMANIA
Red

Premiat Cabernet Sauvignon	about $2

White

Premiat Reisling	about $2

SOVIET UNION
White

Nazdorovya Extra Brut Champagne	about $13

GREECE
Red

Demestica Red, Achaia Claus	about $2

White

Nicolaou Mavrodaphne, Sweet	about $3

Rosé

Rodytis Rosé	about $2

ISRAEL
Red

Carmel Selected Cabernet Sauvignon	about $4

White

Carmel Sauvignon Blanc	about $3

SOUTH AFRICA
Red

KWV Paarl Pinotage	about $4

Sherry

KWV Paarl Sherry	about $4

CHILE
Red

Undurraga Cabernet	about $3
Concha y Toro Reserve Cabernet	about $3

White

Santa Rita Riesling	about $2

ARGENTINA
Red

Andean Vineyards Cabernet	about $3

White

Trumpeter Riesling	about $2

AUSTRALIA
Red

Orlando Hermitage	about $2
Hardy's Cabernet Sauvignon	about $5

White

Seppelt Arawatta Riesling	about $2

CHINA
White

Great Wall	about $6

A
WINE
LOVER'S
GUIDE

HOW TO SERVE WINE

The enjoyment of wine does not call for elaborate equipment. The only necessities are a corkscrew and wineglasses. As for the etiquette of serving, a few common-sense guidelines will suffice.

The variety of corkscrews and other devices for extracting a cork from a bottle can be bewildering, but if the following requirements are met, the tool will work well: the bore—or "worm"—of a good corkscrew should be at least 2¼ inches long; otherwise it will not penetrate far enough into the long cork that seals fine wines. The metal should be fashioned in a true open spiral with smooth, rounded edges. Corkscrews with sharp-edged worms can literally tear up a cork—and still fail to remove it. A corkscrew's leverage should also be considered. Some people prefer the simple T-bar instrument, which offers no mechanical advantage. Loosening a stubborn cork with one of these corkscrews may require all your might. A better device from this standpoint is the double-action one: the top handle screws the bore into the cork, and turning the bottom handle smoothly pulls out even the most obstinate cork. Another good corkscrew, available almost everywhere, has two side arms that rise as the bore spirals into the cork; when these two arms, or levers, are pushed back down against the neck of the bottle, the cork is eased out. A waiter's corkscrew has excellent leverage and folds conveniently into the pocket or handbag for picnicking or traveling.

Before using any corkscrew, remove the protective foil (known as the capsule) around the top of the bottle to well below the lip, since contact with the metal may spoil the taste of the wine. If there is any mold or deposit on the top of the cork and the lip, after extracting the cork wipe the lip of the bottle with a clean napkin or paper towel.

After the bottle is opened, the next thing to consider is the wineglass. Expensive, elegant crystal may be beautiful, but it is not essential. A stemmed clear glass sets off a wine's clarity and color most effectively. The roundness of the bowl enhances the play of light, and the stem makes it possible to hold the goblet without warming the wine or smudging the glass. The colored glasses once in vogue masked the cloudiness of imperfectly clarified wines—a good reason for avoiding them.

Wineglasses come in all shapes and sizes. Many are traditionally paired with a particular wine—for example, the ones with small, clear, rounded bowls supported by tapered colored stems used for German wines. Several styles that are very popular actually interfere with the enjoyment of the wine they are intended for. A case in point is the saucer-shaped champagne glass: its broad, shallow bowl quickly dissipates the delightful bubbles that the winemaker has taken such pains to produce. A slender flute-shaped glass, one that conserves the effervescence, is best for serving champagne.

A simple and ample goblet of clear glass is suitable for any wine. Probably the ideal all-purpose glass is the graceful "tulip" shape, with bowl curved inward at the rim so that it concentrates and retains the wine's bouquet. Generous capacity—eight to ten ounces at least—is essential,

145

because a glass should never be more than one-third filled. The extra space permits swirling the wine about, releasing bouquet and flavor just before it is sipped.

When more than one wine is served, glasses of different sizes may be used. If you are offering both red and white wines, reserve the larger glass for the red, or in the case of two reds, for the older, bigger wine. If you are serving two whites, the older, bigger one is also served in the larger glass.

One other important item is a decanter. Aside from being an attractive appurtenance that will enhance your table, a decanter has a practical advantage. When you pour wine into a decanter you eliminate the chance of finding unpleasant sediment in a glass. While sediment in the bottle is a natural, normally harmless deposit, an indication that the wine has aged properly, no one wants to drink it. (Young wines or wines that have been stabilized so that they will keep longer once they are opened do not throw sediment.)

Decanting is not a difficult procedure. Allow the bottle to stand upright until the sediment has settled to the bottom. This may take as long as a day, certainly not less than three hours. Decant in a good light, one that allows you to see the wine moving inside the bottle. A lighted candle placed behind the neck has been the tradition, but an electric lamp will do just as well. Handling the bottle carefully so as not to disturb the deposit, pour the wine slowly and continuously into the decanter until you see the first bit of sediment in the bottle's neck. Then stop pouring at once. If you have poured slowly and steadily, the sediment will not appear until the very end of the process, and you will lose only about an ounce of wine.

Decanting offers another advantage: aerating the wine as it is poured. The beneficial aeration that occurs in the process of decanting is actually an accelerated form of letting a wine "breathe." Except for the frailest of old vintages, every wine improves if it is given some time to air. Having been cooped up in a bottle for any number of years, a wine needs the opportunity to open up, to bloom, before it can reveal its fullest flavor and bouquet. Red wines, even when not decanted, are opened for a while before serving. Great red and white wines should be given more of a chance to breathe than common ones, but breathing should not be carried to the extreme, lest fragrance and flavor dissipate before the wine is poured. It is certainly better to serve a wine that has not been given enough exposure to the air than one that has stood open too long.

The basic rule in regard to temperature is simple: serve white wines chilled and red wines at room temperature. However, there is a little more to it in some instances. In the first place, what is "room temperature"? It is the temperature of the room in which the wine will be served, ideally about 68 degrees. In Europe it might be closer to 65 degrees, in the United States to 72 degrees. In any case, a red wine brought up from a 55-degree cellar needs an hour or so to come up to the temperature of the dining room, a temperature that shows the qualities of the wine to better advantage than does the cellar's. Some red wines, especially those that have been stored in a warm place, are pleasanter if served slightly cool. Fifteen or twenty minutes in the refrigerator for your Beaujolais or light Spanish red is all that is necessary.

White wines should be cold, but not too cold. Severe chilling can mask the defects in an inferior wine, but a fine white wine numbed to near freezing is robbed of its flavor. Half an hour in a bucket of ice cubes and water or 2½ hours in the refrigerator will properly chill almost any white wine.

HOW TO BUILD A LIBRARY OF WINES

The term "wine cellar" brings to mind some dark, cool, well-stocked cave in the nether regions of a great and opulent house. Of these actual cellars quite a few still exist, impressive in the size and quality of wine collections stored in them, not to mention the investment they represent.

In this day and age, storing wine at home seems as reasonable and agreeable as ever, but "cellar" is no longer the right word. More and more people are building what might better be called "libraries" of wine. Even the smallest apartment can accommodate a modest but select collection of wines. And for people having multiple homes—an apartment in the city, a weekend cottage in the country, and perhaps a *pied-à-terre* abroad—establishing a small but carefully stocked wine library in each makes a great deal of sense. People who know and enjoy wine want to have it on hand to share with friends at a moment's notice or simply when the urge seizes them to enjoy a particular favorite.

Having your own collection of wines, replenished and enlarged as knowledge increases and new discoveries are made, can be a continuing source of gratification. For the wine lover, the labels on the bottles have a special romance, and as the names roll over the tongue they evoke the delight of anticipation—Haut-Brion, Montrachet, Schloss Vollrads, Lafite-Rothschild—names rich in history, tradition, grandeur. Sharing this heritage is part of the intelligent appreciation of wine, clearly one of the civilized pleasures of life.

Aside from the aesthetic and emotional satisfactions, there are practical advantages in building a wine library. One, already mentioned, is the convenience of enjoying a bottle whenever the impulse strikes, or when friends drop by. In your own home you may leisurely make a choice to suit your mood and menu.

Many people feel uncomfortable serving wine because they are afraid of making a mistake or appearing unsophisticated. Never fear. Most wine shibboleths are nonsense. You can ignore them with propriety and proceed with assurance in cultivating your own tastes and preferences. Following are my suggestions for acquiring a well-rounded library of wines, consisting of about fifty bottles that represent the leading winegrowing regions of the world. At 1977 prices, the initial cost would be approximately $275.

Red Bordeaux: '66, '67, '70, '71, '73, '75. Six bottles. Look for fine recognizable districts such as Médoc and Saint-Émilion. More specific and therefore generally better are château-bottled clarets. If the First Growths are too costly, try some relatively reasonable alternatives: Bouscaut (Graves), Figeac (Saint-Émilion), Vieux-Château-Certan (Pomerol), Lynch-Bages (Pauillac).

White Bordeaux: '67, '69, '70, '71, '75. Three bottles. Choose Sauternes and Barsac as sweet dessert wines and Graves as a moderately dry white wine.

Beaujolais: '76. Two bottles. Here is one of the good country wines of France, the younger the better. Look for the *Grand Cru* village wines such as Brouilly and Fleurie.

Red Burgundy: '71, '72, '73, '76. Six bottles. Ask your wine merchant to give you estate-bottlings. The famed vineyards may be too high-priced, so look for such good values as Côtes de Beaune-Villages, Pinot Noir, and Chassagne-Montrachet Rouge.

White Burgundy: '73, '75, '76. Four bottles. These are the dry white glories of France. Select among the better villages such as Chassagne- or Puligny-Montrachet, Meursault, Chablis, and Pouilly-Fuissé. Here, too, look for estate-bottlings.

Rhine and Moselle: '71, '75, '76. Six bottles. Some of the greatest white wines of the world are produced here. Pick '71s for rich and long-lived classics and '73s for quick-maturing, lighter wines. Popular Liebfraumilch is not to be relied upon unless bottled by a reputable shipper. You will be rewarded by asking for the hard-to-pronounce but wonderful wines that bear the names of a town and a vineyard—such wines as Niersteiner Orbel, Rauenthaler Baiken, and Zeltinger Himmelreich.

Country Wines of Europe: Recent vintages. Eight bottles. These wines are fun: delightful and often not expensive, providing a real tasting adventure. Choose among Muscadet, Sancerre, Vouvray, and Pouilly-Fumé from the Loire Valley; Riesling and Gewürztraminer from Alsace; Châteauneuf-du-Pape and Hermitage Rouge from the Rhône (these will need bottle aging); Rioja red and white from Spain; the red Chianti, Valpolicella, and Valtellina wines and white Soave from Italy; Gumpoldskirchner from Austria; Neuchâtel from Switzerland; Vinhos Verdes and Dãos from Portugal. All easily obtainable.

California Red Wine: Recent vintages. Six bottles. Do not overlook the beautiful red wines of northern California. The best bear the grape names Cabernet Sauvignon, Pinot Noir, and Gamay.

American White Wine: Very recent vintages. Six bottles. Excellent examples of dry white wine are grown in northern California and New York State. The best bear the grape name Pinot Chardonnay; other grape names are Riesling, Semillon, Traminer, and Sauvignon Blanc.

Vins Rosés: The most recent vintage. Two bottles. This versatile pink wine adjusts to almost any menu. California rosés are excellent, or choose a moderately priced French one from Tavel, Provence, the Rhône, Bordeaux, or Anjou.

Champagne: Four bottles. The most glamorous of festive drinks is always good to have on hand for anniversaries and birthdays, when it is a must. Select the excellent French nonvintage brut , or try one of the good American champagnes.

Once you have acquired your stock of wines, where will you store them? Actually the question presents no great problem. Any relatively quiet spot in your house or apartment is suitable for a wine rack or shelves, so long as it is free of vibrations and away from direct sunlight. Nor should it be situated near heating or cooling units, where temperature fluctuations can be sharp enough to damage the wines. The ideal "cellar" temperature is between 55 and 60 degrees, but any constant reading below 75 degrees will not hurt wines kept for a reasonable period of time. Remember that wine kept at 70 degrees matures faster than wine stored at 55 degrees.

Wines can be stored in any type of arrangement that suits your fancy. You can keep the finest wines in their commercial cartons, or cases, or on home-crafted shelves. The important consideration in storing wines is that the bottles rest on their sides, tilted slightly, neck down, to keep the corks moist. If a cork dries out and contracts, letting air into the bottle, the wine oxidizes, and eventually spoils completely. Fortified wines such as sherry can stand upright without suffering harm.

A CHART OF RECENT VINTAGE YEARS

The vintage chart is a helpful guide for those wise enough to know when to ignore it. To follow such a chart slavishly, buying nothing but the very greatest of vintage years, means paying the highest prices for the top-rated years and overlooking wines produced in good average years that can be acquired at relatively modest cost. One must put a vintage chart in perspective in order to be able to interpret and grasp its implications. Since some highly touted years may prove not to hold up with the passage of time, constant reevaluation is called for.

This guide was compiled in 1976, and its recommendations should be considered in terms of that year; for example, wines suggested for "present drinking" in 1976 would be good to drink only until 1979 or 1980.

The ratings listed below, which run from 0 to 20 (a vintage given 17 or more is a great one indeed), are offered in the spirit of the British army maxim attributed to Winston Churchill: "Rules are made for the obedience of fools and the guidance of wise men."

RED BORDEAUX

1976 Dry, hot summer spell gave potential of true greatness, but autumn rain diluted result. Rich in color, fruity, but not as concentrated as the classic '75s. — **18**

1975 Big, rich, tannic wines, slow to mature. A very great year. — **20**

1974 A wonderfully dry and sunny summer gave promise of a very special year. September rains dampened these hopes, but they could not completely spoil the wines. In each of the famous districts the wines have good color and will mature well, resembling the lovely '62s and '67s. — **17**

1973 Record-breaking harvest—the largest in thirty years. Because of abundance, wines relatively light, early-maturing, not destined to be long-lived. Wines from the famed châteaus exhibit softness, elegance, and good fruit, with a life expectancy of about 10 years. — **16**

1972 Opening prices broke all records, quality was called high, but the wines have not lived up to early expectations. Insufficient fruit emphasizes the relatively dry, tannic quality on the palate. The austere Cabernet Sauvignon grape thrived, while the softer Merlot did not; hence the Médoc, where Cabernet flourishes, produced better wines than did Saint-Émilion and Pomerol. — **15**

1971 Overlooked because of universal praise showered on the '70s, the '71s may ultimately prove their equal; in many instances they will outlive the '70s. Body, power, and — **19**

fullness are recognizable features. Low yields meant concentrated flavor. Will mature slowly and gracefully.

1970 Shares with '45 and '61 the honor of being among the very best vintages since World War II. Considering the excellence, quantity produced was surprisingly large. Fully developed Merlot grapes added soft and round elegance. Holds promise of long life. 20

1969 Highly praised immediately after the harvest, the '69s are simply not in the league with the '61s, '66s, and '70s. Nevertheless, a most acceptable year, producing excellent, slow-maturing wines, particularly in the Médoc and Graves, with slightly lower quality in Pomerol and Saint-Émilion. The crop was half the normal size. 16

1968 Wines below average in general, but among the better vineyards some are very attractive, and attractively priced. Latour and Haut-Brion, noted for their quality in off years, are especially good values. 12

1967 Bounteous crop; wines show good fruit and balance. Excellent for present drinking and until at least '78. 17

1966 Glorious wines of exceptional bouquet, with superb balance and style. A bit lighter in body than the '61s, but still sufficiently tannic to provide happy drinking until 1995. Worth laying down. 19

1965 Has passed its peak; should be ignored. 2

1964 Charming, fruity wines reaching their apex in Saint-Émilion, Pomerol, and Graves. Unfortunately, rain hit during mid-harvest in the Médoc, drenching about half the vineyards. One must choose carefully here. While awaiting the glories of '66 and '70, the '64s, which can be drunk now, offer much pleasure, and will until 1980. 16

1963 A very spotty year, owing to spells of bad weather. Forget about Saint-Émilion and Pomerol. Some good wines were produced in the Médoc, but most have passed their prime. 9

1962 Overlooked at first, the outstanding qualities of the firm, well-balanced, soft '62s are beginning to be recognized. Good fruit and fine bouquet have developed beautifully. If you can obtain them, you will find them excellent for drinking during the next few years. 16

1961 In the classic tradition of the '45s: low yield, hence well-nourished grapes. Rich concentration, exceptional color, body, and bouquet. Remarkable longevity—some of the wines will be vibrant well into the next century. 20

Older Clarets. The '60s were better than average, but they have not lasted. 1959 was highly acclaimed as "the year of the century"; many of these wines are just at their peak, though some of the lesser vineyards have begun to decline. The '57s continue to be rather hard and disappointing. The '55s are still perfection if properly stored and provide exceptional tasting experience. Fine '53s are still to be found, but we suggest that you try

YEAR		RATING

a bottle before investing in a case. Superb '52s from Saint-Émilion and the Médoc are available. The '50s received little attention, but wines from the top vineyards can be remarkable; '49s from the best châteaus are now glorious. Many '48s are still enjoyable and represent good values, particularly Médocs and Pomerols. If they have been lovingly cared for, '47s offer memorable drinking. The unsurpassed '45s are still dramatically great. Among the older claret vintages that have retained their excellence and character are '37, '34, '29, '28, '24, '23, '21, and '18. If properly cared for and decanted, they can provide extraordinary moments. Anything older than 1918 is uncertain.

WHITE BORDEAUX

1976 Graves dry, irregular, varying from vineyard to vineyard. Sauternes rich, sweet, remarkable—the equal of the great '75s. — 17

1975 Excellent in Sauternes, and nearly as good for dry white Graves. — 18

1974 Good average year for both Sauternes and Graves. — 16

1973 Both fruit and balance poor in Sauternes. — 11
Graves are somewhat better but not outstanding. — 14

1972 Though striking a fine balance of fruit and acidity, the Graves are a bit light and thin. — 16
Here again, Sauternes did not get its full quota of October sunshine and the wines are disappointing. — 13

1971 Graves well-balanced, possessing depth and an appealing style, fresh bouquet and flavor. — 18

YEAR		RATING

In Sauternes, beautiful fruit and perfect balance have given us rich and elegant wines. Equals the great '62. — 19

1970 A bounteous vintage in Graves, producing very fine wines, medium-dry with charming fruit. — 18
Excellent, concentrated richness in Sauternes means wines of velvet smoothness, luscious fruit, and long life. — 17

1969 Graves excellent in their early years but now beginning to show age. — 14
Rather poor overall quality in Sauternes, but d'Yquem stands supreme. — 10-16

1968 No wines of distinction. — 10

1967 Good, well-made, attractive Graves. — 16
Sauternes outstanding, rich and deep, long-lived. — 19

Older White Bordeaux. Sauternes and Barsac reached glorious heights in 1962, with '61 and '59 not far behind, if not equal. The wines of these vintages will last for many years to come. Sweet wines from the best châteaus can still be enjoyed in these classic vintages: '55, '53, '49, '45, '37, '34, '21, "18, '14, and '08. The dry whites of Graves are too old if they bear a date before 1969.

RED BURGUNDY

1976 Earliest harvest in modern memory. Weather, unlike Bordeaux's, held throughout picking. Reds rich, full, long-lived, with practically no sugaring required to increase alcohol. Truly great. — 20

1975 Hopes for an excellent vintage — 8–14

YEAR	RATING

were dashed by a wet and humid September. Wines from the hillsides are acceptable, those from the low-lying vineyards are not.

1974 Like Bordeaux, Burgundy looked forward to a splendid vintage, but the cool, wet weather of September resulted in wines that were good, not great. Average quantity, much less than in the record year of 1973. — 11–17

1973 A record crop, as in Bordeaux, with wines of medium quality. Many of the lesser wines are thin and watery. Careful consideration is required to select the best wines from the good vineyards. These will mature rather quickly and can be enjoyed fairly young. — 8–17

1972 Very firm wines of strong character, depth, and balance. Not so harsh as originally thought, but the abundance of tannin means the wines will live long. Slow-maturing, worth waiting for. Many excellent smaller wines. — 18

1971 Possibly the best red Burgundies since 1929. Very complete wines, possessing all the richness, power, and depth for which the wines of Burgundy are renowned. Sufficient fruit to give them a gentle roundness as well. Will last for twenty years. — 20

1970 Well-balanced, stylish wines produced in great quantity. Superb for drinking now and over the next few years. — 15

1969 An extraordinary year, with wines rich in tannin needing many years to develop. Unfortunately, many of the great wines have already been consumed, since this was a very small vintage. Fine for drinking from the late 1970s on. — 19

YEAR	RATING

1968 The worst Burgundy vintage in two decades. — 8

1967 Though some good examples can be found, most '67 Burgundies proved too light and pale, vanishing quickly on the palate. — 12

1966 A very good year, with fruity, elegant wines, especially fine as to bouquet. They are not long-lived and some may be over the hill, but the better wines are at their peak now. — 17

1965 Forget about this one.

1964 Many of the best wines have matured slowly and well and are close to their prime. Though originally touted as remarkable, some of the wines have already lost their fruit and attractiveness. Careful choice is necessary. — 14–18

1963 Poor. — 9

1962 The well-made wines from superior vineyards are extremely pleasing to drink now; the others, lacking fruit and depth, are disappointing. — 16

1961 Superb wines of great longevity. Now just coming around and will be great for at least ten years— until 1987. Few remain, owing to the very small harvest. — 19

Older Burgundies. As a rule, red Burgundy does not last more than a decade, though time and time again the top vineyards are the exceptions that prove the rule. The '59s were uniformly superb, but most are old and tired. A few fine '52s and '49s can still provide dramatic drinking.

WHITE BURGUNDY

1976 Biggest, fattest Burgundies since — 19

YEAR		RATING

1959. Dramatic for three or four years, but will not live long because of lack of acidity.

1975 Best since 1969. The whites were not affected by the rot that ruined the reds. Good Chablis. — 18

1974 Light and simple wines, on the average, but with some very fine ones produced at the famous vineyards. — 15

1973 Last-minute rains produced a bountiful crop but filled the grapes with water. The resulting wines are fruity, supple, and graceful but very light, and should be consumed young. — 15–17

1972 Cooler weather made most Chablis excessively acid. Select carefully. — 10–15

1971 The whites from the Côte d'Or, farther south, will be elegant until 1980. Though rich and nectarlike, the wines are not long-lived. Should be enjoyed now. — 17

1970 Graceful and fruity, these wines have developed quickly and are ideal for drinking now. Fine balance of fruit, alcohol, and acidity. — 18

1969 As with the reds, greatness was achieved here. Quite rich wines, possibly the best white Burgundy in several decades, but very limited quantity. — 19

Older White Burgundies. The life expectancy of white Burgundy is not great, so it is best not to get involved with anything older than 1969, though the remarkable wines of 1961, if from the top vineyards, are still enjoyable.

BEAUJOLAIS

Vintage years do not mean much when the label reads simply

YEAR		RATING

"Beaujolais" or "Beaujolais Villages." These light, fruity wines should be consumed when their charm is greatest—in their youth, usually within two years of the vintage. But the nine *Grand Cru* Beaujolais, such as Fleurie and Brouilly, may ripen beautifully in three to six years after bottling. Many of these are well worth waiting for. Since lesser Beaujolais do not live long, avoid anything older than 1971.

1976 Rich, full, high alcohol—in the grand Beaujolais tradition of '61 and '71. Good fruit and acidity. Wines from the better vineyards, such as Brouilly, will be long-lived. — 19

1975 In the low-lying vineyards of ordinary Beaujolais, a disaster similar to Burgundy proper, but good wines from the hillside appellations (Brouilly, Juliénas, etc.). — 8–16

1974 A very large crop of pleasant, fruity wines. As always, the wines from the nine *Crus* made the best Beaujolais. — 17

1973 A huge crop, which produced thin wines in some cases, though the *Grands Crus* made the most of their hilltop situations and produced typically fruity, delightful Beaujolais to be enjoyed within the next three years. — 13–17

1972 A very disappointing vintage for Beaujolais fans. Though there were some superb exceptions in Brouilly and Moulin-à-Vent, most wines were lacking in fruit, the heartthrob of Beaujolais. — 12–16

1971 A most unusual year in Beaujolais, — 18

153

YEAR		RATING

with wines high in tannin and long on depth. They taste amazingly like the lighter reds of the Côte d'Or. Classic, long-lived Beaujolais.

CÔTES DU RHÔNE

1976 Reds, because of the hot summer, are powerful and high in alcohol. Outstanding successes, from Châteauneuf-du-Pape in the south to Côte Rôtie in the north. — 19

1975 Spotty, with rainy weather resulting in poor wines for many growers. Châteauneuf-du-Pape was mediocre. — 8–16

1974 Sizable production of average-quality wines. Choose carefully. — 11–16

1973 A record-breaking crop, of which 20 percent is truly excellent. For the rest, excessive production diluted quality. — 12–17

1972 Excellent wines, generous in body, depth, and character. Big and long-lived. — 19

1971 Limited quantity and uneven quality because of rain during the harvest. A few good wines, but select with care. — 14–17

1970 A hot, dry summer and fine weather during the harvest gave uniformly excellent wines. Good quantity; round, strong character. — 19

1969 Fine wines throughout the Rhône Valley; not a large production, but good flavor and bouquet. — 18

1968 Fared much better than the rest of France during this year. Some very agreeable wines. — 14

1967 Reds are very attractive for present drinking. — 16

Whites and rosés were disappointing; most are now too old. — 12

1966 Superb, especially Hermitage and Châteauneuf-du-Pape, both with fine balance and longevity. Very charming wines. — 18

The whites of the region were also excellent. The rosés are too old. — 17

Older Côtes du Rhône. Some red wines of the Côtes du Rhône have great longevity. The wines of '62 are fine for drinking now. The remarkable '61s, the best postwar vintage on the Rhône, are wines of beautiful balance and charming fruit. Excellent now and for years to come. You would indeed be fortunate to come upon '57, '53, '49, or '45—dramatically great wines. They will have thrown much sediment and should be decanted carefully.

LOIRE VALLEY

1976 Generous sunshine resulted in an early harvest, yielding perhaps the best Loire whites during this generation. All wines, including Muscadet, Pouilly-Fumé and Sancerre, are outstanding. A year to pay attention to in the Loire. — 20

1975 A very good vintage, from Pouilly and Sancerre to Muscadet. Fruity, full and complete. — 18

1974 Good wines generally, but no great peaks. — 15

1973 Typically fresh and charming wines throughout the valley, to be drunk with pleasure while still young. — 18

1972 The grapes did not ripen properly in most areas, and the resulting wines were thin and rather acid. Muscadet, where the nearby At- — 13–16

YEAR   RATING

lantic Ocean moderated the otherwise cool season, was the exception, giving lovely wines.

1971 Small production but full, well-ripened wines of delectable fragrance. Longer-lived than most recent Loire vintages, they will provide pleasant drinking until 1981 or 1982.   **18**

1970 Certainly one of the best vintages in two decades. Stylish wines with appealing bouquet and dryness, attractive for drinking now.   **19**

Older Vintages. For the most part, the charm of Loire wines is their youthful freshness and fruit. There are exceptions, however, among the very sweet wines of Anjou and Vouvray, some of which in great vintages can be very long-lived indeed. The reds of Chinon and Bourgueil improve after a few years in bottle.

CHAMPAGNE

Vintages are declared in Champagne only when the harvest results in particularly excellent wines. Most champagne, however, is a blend of the wines of several years and thus cannot bear a vintage date. The great vintages ready to drink now are '72, '71, '70, '69, '66, '64, '61, and (if stored properly) '59, '55, and '52. Shippers in Champagne claim that 1976 holds great promise for the future.

ALSACE

1976 Early harvest, outstanding quality—may even surpass the classic 1971 vintage.   **19**

YEAR   RATING

1975 Excellent wines with much style and grace.   **18**

1974 Normal quantity, good quality, better than the '73s. The best should be given some bottle aging.   **17**

1973 High yield of light, fruity, agreeable, typically Alsatian wines.   **17**

1972 Less fruit and more acidity than 1973. Refreshing.   **14**

1971 As in Germany, its neighbor across the Rhine, a truly outstanding vintage. Wines are extremely rich, full, and fruity.   **19**

1970 Record-breaking crop of light and early-maturing wines.   **15**

Older Vintages. Save for a few rare exceptions, wine from Alsace older than 1970 should be avoided.

RHINE AND MOSELLE

1976 Lightning strikes twice! 1975 reached new heights in excellence, only to be surpassed by 1976. Hot sun has made practically all Rhines and Moselles rich, fruity, concentrated and dramatic. Virtually no ordinary, light dry wines are produced—only giants.   **20**

1975 In exalted league of '71; rich in fruit, depth. Superb balance, great longevity.   **19**

1974 Rain during the harvest along the Rhine and the Moselle prevented both estates and cooperatives from producing the better grades of wine: little *Auslese* will be seen. Average quantity of light, quick-to-mature wines.   **15**

1973 As in France, nature was bounteous, making probably the largest vintage ever harvested in Germany. Elegant, light, and of fine   **17**

155

YEAR		RATING

fruitiness, the wines will be enjoyable at least through 1978.

1972 Essentially light, pleasant wines for consuming early. Not for laying down. **14**

1971 An exceedingly great year, in the same exalted class as '53, '45, and '37. Much rich *Spätlese* and *Auslese* was produced, all possessed of beautiful balance and longevity. Here are wines that can be enjoyed through 1985 as complexity develops in the bottle. **20**

1970 Light, typical wines produced in large quantity. The better ones, to the surprise of many, will still be delightful even at the end of the 1970s. **16**

1969 Pleasant enough until 1973, but now too old. **12**

1968 Fine body and style and an adequate balance between sugar and acidity, but few great rich wines were produced. **12–15**

1967 Good balance and depth; many superb *Auslese* wines that will be very long-lived. **18**

1966 High average quality, some wines with great finesse. Not for laying down after 1975. **15**

Older German White Wines. Surprisingly, the best *Auslese* wines of '53 and '59 are still superb and will delight us until 1985. Wines older than '53 should be ignored.

ITALY

Until recently, there was little control of the vintage dates appearing on bottles of Italian wine. In 1963 the Italian government created the *Denominazione di Origine Controllata*, the Italian counterpart of the French *Appellation Contrôlée*. Stricter standards, more precise language, and tasting tests, all administered by local wine committees, now enable us to rely on the vintage dates appearing on Italian wine labels. It must be remembered that most Italian wines are quick-maturing, informal, meant to be drunk young—in many instances the younger the better. As a general rule we recommend looking for a very recent vintage date, indicating an age of not over three years, on such wines as Bardolino, Soave, Valpolicella, Verdicchio, Chiaretto, and all wines grown south of Rome.

The better red wines, as in France and California, profit from barrel and bottle aging. Maturation particularly benefits wines made from Nebbiolo grapes grown in Piedmont and Lombardy: Barolo, Barbaresco, Gattinara, Ghemme, and the Valtellina wines Sassella, Inferno, and Grumello. A few years in bottle also improve the finer Chiantis, wines from the heart of Tuscany. The better Chiantis are identified by such adjectives as "Riserva" and "Classico." Avoid the attractive straw-covered bottles. These wines are not the finer grades of Chianti; they have not been aged. Among the recent red-wine vintages to look for are 1975, 1973, 1971, 1970, 1967, 1966, 1964, 1962, and 1961.

SPAIN

For the most part, Spain's Mediterranean climate makes vintage years unimportant. The exception is one small corner of the country near the French border: the Rioja region, about 150 miles southwest of Bordeaux. Here a temperate climate prevails, varying widely from year to year, so that vintage dates take on real meaning. But, unfortunately, Rioja growers revere age for its own sake, and some of the Reservas spend too many years in barrel, losing freshness. Many wise producers now bottle closer to the vintage date, and this trend bodes well for the future of Rioja wines. Outstanding recent vintages are 1975, 1973, 1971, 1969, 1966, 1964, 1962, and 1961. Despite tales of legendary high-priced wines, it is hazardous to venture into years earlier than 1961. As for the rest of the table wines of Spain, the most recent vintage is to be preferred.

PORTUGAL

With the important exception of Vintage Port, the Portuguese solve the tricky vintage problem by dating few of their wines. Vinhos Verdes, Rosés, Dãos, and Colares are wines to quaff informally, for pleasure is to be found in their young charm.

As for Vintage Port, the year on the label is all-important. The wines mature slowly indeed, never revealing their excellence until at least a decade has passed. If you are lucky enough to find them, the following vintages can be enjoyed now and many years hence: 1960, 1958, 1955, 1950, 1948, 1945. Port for laying down should be chosen from 1973, 1970, 1966, and 1963.

CALIFORNIA

From Repeal up until about 1954 California vintners boasted, "In Europe there are good and bad vintages, in California only good ones," and vintage dating was scorned as unnecessary and unimportant. Now, however, wiser wine men have learned that there is no fine table wine district anywhere in the world that is not subject to variable weather patterns affecting the quality of the wine. Today we can compare a great Napa Cabernet Sauvignon for 1973 with the same wine from 1972, a year of distinctly inferior quality.

If you have ever tasted a fine ten-year-old Cabernet Sauvignon, you will realize that the better California wines develop in bottle the way a Château Margaux or a Château Haut-Brion does. One of the wisest wine investments is a 1973 Napa or Sonoma Cabernet acquired young, while the cost is low. Let it rest in your cellar for several years, to be drunk only when it has aged properly. By that time the same wine will command triple the price—if available at all.

Unlike Europe, California does not experience really disastrous vintages. Nevertheless, some years are better than others. Among the better recent years are 1975, 1973, 1971, 1970, 1969, 1968, and 1966.

Drought in the winter/spring of 1976, followed by heavy September rains, reduced the harvest to less than half of normal in northern California. However, because of concentration, the Napa/Sonoma wine will be full-bodied and long-lived.

NEW YORK STATE

It is difficult to discuss vintages in New York unless we are sure that everything in the bottle was grown within the confines of the state. Such smaller vineyards as Bully Hill, Benmarl, Vinifera Vineyards, and a few of the large producers make 100 percent New York wine. For these the following vintage ratings hold true: 1975, 1973, 1971, and 1967 were excellent years for both red and white wines, thanks to especially good weather in the late summer and fall. 1972 made better white than red wines; 1970 finer reds than whites.

WINE AND FOOD AFFINITIES

One of the great pleasures in planning a meal is choosing wines and foods that balance each other.

There are time-ravaged rules about wine and food, of course, which many wine lovers still feel are inviolable, but we have reached an age where individuality and informality are winning out over the old conventions. We are more adventurous about our eating and drinking than we used to be, and this attitude is shared by increasing numbers of young people. Rules about wine are really pretty simple if they are applied with common sense. The basic maxim goes: a white wine before a red wine, a light wine before a full wine, a dry wine before a sweet wine, and a young wine before an old wine. Well, I think any person with a sense of balance in eating and drinking would naturally arrive at these ideas. If it's true that you try to build your menu to a climax, course by course, why wouldn't you choose the wines in an ascending order to set it off? It's logical.

The following chart indicates some of the traditional pairings of wine and food. In most cases alternatives are offered that should lead you toward some creative experiments of your own.

Food	*Suggested Wines or Spirits*
Caviar	Brut champagne, vodka, Zubrowka.
Hors d'oeuvres such as crudités, olives, almonds, deviled eggs, smoked salmon	Dry aperitifs such as Fino or Amontillado sherry, Sercial or Rainwater Madeira, Lillet Blonde, Montilla, Manzanilla.
Meat pâtés and foie gras	Sometimes in France foie gras is accompanied by Sauternes very chilled (which reduces the sweetness). Interesting alternatives are cooled Beaujolais, a light red Bordeaux, Zinfandel, and Gamay, all of which admirably suit a meat pâté. If a full-bodied dry white is to be served with the following course, it would also be satisfactory here.
Consommé	Dry sherry or Madeira.
Fish soups, chowders	A light crisp white, such as Soave, Alsatian or California Riesling, Muscadet, Manzanilla, or Montilla.
Cream soups	Same as for the preceding, though a heavier white wine from the Loire is preferable.
Cold meats and other light fare for a summer picnic or buffet	Light dry wine such as Moselle, vin rosé, slightly chilled Beaujolais, Valpolicella, or Spanish Rioja.

Eggs, cheese, or stuffed omelet	Light red such as Zinfandel or a regional Médoc; perhaps a Tavel or a Grenache Rosé.
Cheese dishes, such as quiche Lorraine, fondues	Crisp dry white such as Alsatian Riesling or Swiss Neuchâtel.
Pasta	With seafood sauce—Soave or Verdicchio; with meat sauce—Chianti Riserva.
Shellfish	Chablis, white Graves, Muscadet, California or New York Riesling.
Fish, poached or grilled	Same as for the preceding; also Pouilly-Fuissé, Rheingau, Moselle.
Fish in heavy sauce or seafood ragout	Any full white Burgundy such as Meursault; a full-flavored Rheingau such as Rüdesheimer; California Pinot Chardonnay.
Chicken or turkey	A full-bodied white (as for the preceding), or a light red Bordeaux, Beaujolais, Bardolino, or Cabernet Sauvignon.
Ham and pork	Neither really complements great wine. Fruity white or sparkling wines are pleasant (champagne with ham).
Veal, sweetbreads, brains, tripe, etc.	Full-bodied white Burgundy, light red Bordeaux, California Cabernet Sauvignon, Côtes du Rhône, Beaujolais (Moulin à-Vent).
Lamb	The classic choice is château-bottled Bordeaux (or California Cabernet Sauvignon).
Beef, light game such as quail or pheasant	Fuller-bodied red Bordeaux (such as Saint-Émilion), California Pinot Noir, Côtes de Beaune red, Chianti Classico, hearty Rhône.
Light stews (veal, lamb, or chicken)	Medium light wines such as Beaujolais, Zinfandel, Côtes du Rhône, Barbera, Volnay.
Heavier stews, cooked with wine	Châteauneuf-du-Pape, Hermitage, Côte de Nuits, Burgundy, Barolo, California Pinot Noir.
Heavier game — venison, wild duck, goose,	Full-bodied red—one of the bigger Burgundies or Rhône wines.
Salad	None, unless lemon or cognac is substituted for vinegar.
Cheese	The finest Bordeaux, Burgundies, Rhônes, vintage California Cabernet, Pinot Noir. Also fine old ports. All wines are flattered by cheese—the bigger the wine, the better the mating.
Desserts, fruits, pastries	Château d'Yquem and German *Trockenbeerenauslese.* because of their sweet, flowery qualities, represent perfection, but try also the richest, sweetest examples you can find from Sauternes, the Loire, the Rhine and Moselle; Tokay, Madeira, champagne.
Walnuts, special cheeses such as Stilton or Cheddar	Port, Madeira (Malmsey or Bual).

WINE BUYERS PRICE LIST

For your convenience, the wines recommended throughout this book in their appropriate sections are grouped in this list in approximate price categories. Included are more than 600 wines from all over the world—109 of them costing about $3.00—all of them enjoyable. Prices will vary somewhat according to vintage year. For comments on which years to seek out and which to avoid, see A Chart of Recent Vintage Years, page 149.

For fuller information on a specific wine see references to text in Index.

AMERICAN WINES

ABOUT $3

Red
Beaulieu Burgundy
Buena Vista Zinfandel
Italian Swiss Colony Zinfandel
Robert Mondavi California Table Wine
Pedroncelli Sonoma County
Sonoma Vineyards Zinfandel
Almadén Monterey Zinfandel
Simi Cabernet Sauvignon
Sebastiani Gamay Beaujolais
Sebastiani Barbera
Sebastiani Cabernet Sauvignon
Monterey Gamay Beaujolais
Monterey Zinfandel
Gallo Hearty Burgundy (magnum)
Franzia Zinfandel (half-gallon)
Guild Vino da Tavola Red (half-gallon)
Guild Winemasters Zinfandel
   (half-gallon)
Boordy Cabernet Sauvignon
Bully Hill Chelois Noir
Tabor Hill Baco Noir
Great Western Baco Noir
Meier's Château Jac-Jan Ohio Valley
   Red
Santo Tomás Cabernet Sauvignon
Château Gai Burgundy

White
Beringer Fumé Blanc
Beringer Johannisberg Riesling
Cuvaison Chenin Blanc
Christian Brothers Chenin Blanc
Foppiano Chenin Blanc
Inglenook Johannisberg Riesling
Inglenook Sauvignon Blanc

Robert Mondavi California Table Wine
Pedroncelli Sonoma County
Sonoma Vineyards Summer Riesling
Oakville Vineyards Our House
Parducci Chenin Blanc
Almadén Monterey Chenin Blanc
Concannon Sauvignon Blanc
Paul Masson Emerald Dry
Paul Masson Chenin Blanc
Monterey Del Mar Ranch
Monterey Chenin Blanc
Mirassou Burgundy
Mirassou Chenin Blanc
Wente Bros. Blanc de Blancs
Wente Bros. Johannisberg Riesling
Gallo Chablis Blanc (magnum)
Guild Vino da Tavola White
   (half-gallon)
Boordy Semillon Sec
Boordy Chenin Blanc
Gold Seal Chablis Nature
Gold Seal Pinot Chardonnay
Bully Hill Aurora Blanc
Great Western Duchess
Taylor Emerald Riesling
Widmer's Delaware
Widmer's Foch
Tarula Farm's White
Isle St. George Dessert Wine
Vermont Vineyards Apple Wine
Ste. Michelle Chenin Blanc
Bright's Pinot Chardonnay

Rosé
Robert Mondavi Gamay
Monterey Grenache Rosé
Franzia Vin Rosé (half-gallon)

ABOUT $5

Red
Beaulieu Beaumont Pinot Noir
Christian Brothers Cabernet Sauvignon
Brother Timothy Zinfandel
Clos du Val Cabernet Sauvignon
Clos du Val Zinfandel
Foppiano Pinot Noir
Grand Cru Zinfandel
Inglenook Pinot Noir
Heitz Cellars Barbera
Charles Krug Cabernet Sauvignon
Souverain Zinfandel
Parducci Gamay Beaujolais
Sutter Home Zinfandel

Yverdon Gamay Beaujolais
Louis M. Martini Barbera
Louis M. Martini Cabernet Sauvignon
Louis M. Martini Pinot Noir
David Bruce Petite Sirah
Simi Pinot Noir
Sebastiani North Coast Pinot Noir
Concannon Petite Sirah
Mirassou Pinot Noir
San Martin Zinfandel
Callaway Zinfandel
Benmarl Baco Noir
Vinifera Cabernet Sauvignon

White
Beaulieu Beaufort Pinot Chardonnay
Freemark Abbey Johannisberg Riesling
Cuvaison Pinot Chardonnay
Chappellet Chenin Blanc
Chappellet Johannisberg Riesling
Christian Brothers Napa Fumé
Heitz Cellars Gewürztraminer
Robert Mondavi Pinot Chardonnay
Robert Mondavi Fumé Blanc
Sonoma Vineyards Johannisberg
   Riesling
Charles Krug Pinot Chardonnay
Charles Krug Gewürztraminer
Oakville Vineyards Johannisberg
   Riesling
Oakville Vineyards Sauvignon Blanc
Spring Mountain Sauvignon Blanc
Sterling Chenin Blanc
Louis M. Martini Pinot Chardonnay
Chalone Chenin Blanc
Simi Gewürztraminer
Simi Pinot Chardonnay
Concannon Johannisberg Riesling
The Novitiate of Los Gatos Muscat de
   Frontignan
Wente Bros. Pinot Chardonnay
Wente Bros. Johannisberg Riesling
   Spätlese
Callaway Chenin Blanc
Callaway White Riesling
Benmarl Seyval Blanc
Vinifera Gewürztraminer
Vinifera Pinot Chardonnay
Vinifera Johannisberg Riesling
Chicama Vineyards Chardonnay

Rosé
Simi Cabernet Rosé

Sparkling
Beaulieu B.V. Brut
Korbel Brut
Paul Masson Brut
Weibel Brut
Gold Seal Brut
Great Western Brut
Great Western Natural

Fortified

ABOUT $5

Port
Ficklin Tinta Cao
Ficklin Tinta Madera

ABOUT $7

White
Ch. Montelena Chardonnay
Sterling Chardonnay

$8 AND OVER

Red
Ch. Montelena Cabernet Sauvignon
Freemark Abbey Cabernet Sauvignon
Freemark Abbey Cabernet Bosché
Chappellet Cabernet Sauvignon
Inglenook Cabernet Sauvignon Cask
Heitz Cellars Cabernet Sauvignon
Robert Mondavi Cabernet Sauvignon
Oakville Vineyards Cabernet Sauvignon
Hanzell Pinot Noir
Souverain Cabernet Sauvignon
Spring Mountain Cabernet Sauvignon
Sterling Cabernet Sauvignon
Mayacamas Cabernet Sauvignon
Mayacamas Zinfandel
Yverdon Cabernet Sauvignon
Louis M. Martini Cabernet Sauvignon
    Private Reserve
David Bruce Zinfandel
Chalone Pinot Noir
Ridge Zinfandel
Ridge Cabernet Sauvignon
Stag's Leap Cabernet Sauvignon

White
Freemark Abbey Pinot Chardonnay
Heitz Cellars Pinot Chardonnay
Hanzell Pinot Chardonnay
Stony Hill Johannisberg Riesling
Stony Hill Pinot Chardonnay
Spring Mountain Pinot Chardonnay

David Bruce Pinot Chardonnay
Chalone Pinot Chardonnay
Ridge Pinot Chardonnay

Sparkling
Korbel Natural
Sonoma Vineyards Brut
Hanns Kornell Brut
Hanns Kornell Sehr Trocken
Schramsberg Blanc de Blancs
Schramsberg Blanc de Noirs
Mirassou Au Naturel
Chandon Napa Valley Brut
Chandon Cuvée de Pinot Noir

IMPORTED WINES

ABOUT $3

Red
Beaujolais
Côtes du Rhône
Lirac Rouge
Saumur Champigny
Corbières
Fitou
Minervois
Bellet
Côtes de Provence
Bergerac
Valpolicella, Bertani
Grão Vasco Dão
Slovin Cabernet
Adriatica Cabernet Istria
Premiat Cabernet Sauvignon
Demestica Red Achaia Claus
Undurraga Cabernet
Concha y Toro Reserve Cabernet
Andean Vineyards Cabernet
Orlando Hermitage

White
Gros Plant du Pays Nantais
Muscadet
Macon Blanc
Monbazillac
Montravel
Saumur
Savennières
Schloss Graffenegg, Prince von
    Metternich
Gumpoldskirchner Königswein, Count
    George
René Barbier Blanco
Casal Garcia Vinho Verde

Lake Balaton Riesling
Slovin Jerusalem Traminer
Premiat Riesling
Nicolaou Mavrodaphne, Sweet
Carmel Sauvignon Blanc
Santa Rita Riesling
Trumpeter Riesling
Seppelt Arawatta Riesling

Rosé
Lirac Rosé
Cassis (Provence)
Mateus
Rodytis Rosé
Bandol

$3–$7 (depending on vintage)

Red
Ch. Meyney
Ch. Marbuzet
Ch. Les Ormes de Pez
Ch. Phélan Ségur
Ch. Grand-Puy-Ducasse
Ch. Langoa-Barton
Ch. Cantenac-Brown
Ch. Malescot-St.-Exupéry
Ch. Prieuré-Lichine
Ch. Kirwan
Ch. Mouton-Cadet
Pontet-Latour
B & G Prince Noir
Ginestet Haut-Médoc
La Cour Pavillon
Sichel My Cousin's Claret
Lichine Médoc
Sichel St. Émilion
Ch. Brane-Cantenac
Ch. Haut-Bailly
Ch. Malartic-Lagravière
Ch. Chauvin
Ch. Dessault
Ch. Ripeau
Ch. Tertre-Daugay
Ch. Belair
Ch. Canon
Ch. Pavie
Ch. Trottevieille
Côte de Nuits Villages
Côte de Beaune Villages
Beaujolais
Beaujolais Villages
Morgon
Brouilly
Côte de Brouilly

Fleurie
Chénas
Chiroubles
Moulin à Vent
St.-Amour
Juliénas
Côtes du Rhône
Lirac Rouge
Cornas
St.-Joseph
Gigondas
Chinon
Bourgueil
Cahors
Chianti Classico, Nozzole
Marqués de Cáceras
Carmel Selected Cabernet Sauvignon
Egri Bikaver
KWV Paarl Pinotage

White
Ch. Couhins
Ch. Malartic-Lagravière
Ch. Olivier
Ch. Latour-Martillac
Ch. Carbonnieux
Ch. Guiraud
Ch. La Tour Blanche
Ch. Suduiraut
Ch. Rieussec
Ch. Mouton-Cadet
Pontet-Latour
Lichine Graves
Auxey-Duresses
Monthélie
St.-Véran
Chablis
Pouilly-Vinzelles
Pouilly-Loché
Bollinger Still Champagne
Charbaut Still Champagne
Sancerre
Vouvray
Muscadet-sur-Lie
Sylvaner
Riesling
Cassis (Provence)
Crépy
Étoile
Jurançon
Bandol Blanc de Blancs
Rüdesheimer Berg Schlossberg Kabinett
    von Schorlemer
Graacher Himmelreich Kabinett, J. J.
    Prüm
Piesporter Goldtröpfchen Kabinett,
    Viet
Ürziger Würtzgarten Kabinett, Jos.
    Beeres
Deidesheimer Herrgottsacker Kabinett,
    Winzerverein Deidesheim

Orvieto Secco, Ruffino
Soave, Bolla
Verdicchio, Fazi-Battaglia
White Cotnari

Rosé
Tavel
Anjou Rosé de Cabernet

$4–$8 (depending on vintage)

Red
Ch. de Pez
Ch. Lafon-Rochet
Ch. Cos-Labory
Ch. Grand-Puy-Lacoste
Ch. Pontet-Canet
Ch. Duhart-Milon-Rothschild
Ch. Clerc-Milon
Ch. Mouton-Baron-Philippe
Ch. Haut-Batailley
Ch. Gloria
Ch. Talbot
Ch. Beychevelle
Ch. Ducru-Beaucaillou
Ch. Gruaud-Larose
Ch. Léoville-Barton
Ch. Léoville-Las-Cases
Ch. Léoville-Poyferré
Ch. Lascombes
Ch. Giscours
Ch. Rauzan-Gassies
Ch. Rausan-Ségla
Ch. Bouscaut
Ch. Pape-Clément
Ch. Domaine de Chevalier
Ch. La Tour Haut-Brion
Ch. La Gaffelière
Ch. Figeac
Ch. Beauséjour
Ch. l'Angélus
Ch. Troplongue-Mondot
Ch. Gazin
Ch. Lafleur
Ch. Nénin
Ch. Petit-Village
Ch. Rouget
Ch. Trotenoy
Vieux-Château-Certain
Ch. Clinet
Ch. Lagrange
Fixin
Clos Napoléon
Clos de la Perrière
Gevrey-Chambertin
Morey-St. Denis
Chambolle-Musigny
Vougeot
Vosne-Romanée
Nuits-St.-Georges
Porrets
Vaucrains

Pruliers
Auxey-Duresses
Pernand-Vergelesses
Savigny-les-Beaune
Beaune
Côte Rôtie
Hermitage Rouge
Bandol
Barolo, Marchese Spinola

White
Ch. Climens
Ch. Coutet
Pouilly-Fuissé
Chablis:
    Montée de Tonnerre
    Mont de Milieu
    Vaulorent
    Fourchaume
    Côte de Lechet
    Beugnons
    Buttreaux
    Les Forêts
    Montmains
Hermitage Blanc
Pouilly-Fumé
Quart de Chaumes
Bonnezeaux
Côteaux du Layon
Gewürztraminer
Arbois
Schloss Vollrads Blue-Gold Kabinett
Schloss Johannisberg Orange Seal
    Kabinett
Hattenheimer Nussbrunnen Kabinett,
    von Simmern
Rauenthaler Baiken Kabinett, Graf Eltz
Erbacher Marcobrunn Kabinett, von
    Simmern
Steinberger Kabinett State Domain
Berncastler Schlossberg Kabinett Wwe.
    Dr. Thanisch
Josephshofer Kabinett, von Kesselstatt
Niersteiner Hipping Kabinett, Karl L.
    Schmitt
Niersteiner Orbel Kabinett, Franz K.
    Schmitt
Oppenheimer Sackträger Kabinett,
    Senfter
Forster Jesuitengarten Kabinett,
    Bassermann-Jordan
Forster Kirchenstück Kabinett, von
    Buhl

$5–$11 (depending on vintage)

Red
Ch. Cos d'Estournel
Ch. Calon-Ségur
Ch. Montrose
Ch. Lynch-Bages

Ch. Pichon-Longueville-Lalande
Ch. Pichon-Longueville
Sichel Margaux
Ch. Palmer
Ch. La Mission Haut-Brion
Clos Fourtet
Ch. Magdelaine
Ch. La Fleur-Petrus
Clos St. Jacques
Varoilles
Aux Combettes
Chapelle-Chambertin
Charmes Chambertin
Latricières-Chambertin
Ruchottes-Chambertin
Mazy-Chambertin
Mazoyères-Chambertin
Griotte-Chambertin
Clos de la Roche
Clos des Lambrays
Clos de Tart
Amoureuses
Charmes
Malconsort
Suchots
Les St.-George
Corton-Grancey
Clos du Roi (Aloxe Corton)
Greves (Beaune)
Feves (Beaune)
Cras (Beaune)
Clos des Mouches (Beaune)
Pommard
   Rugiens
   Épenots
Volnay
   Caillerets
   Clos des Chênes
   Clos des Ducs
Châteauneuf-du-Pape
Spanna Campi Raudii, Vallana
Chianti Riserva Ducale, Ruffino
Marqués de Murrieta
Marqués de Riscal
Dôle du Mont
Hardy's Cabernet Sauvignon

White
Ch. Bouscaut-Blanc
Ch. Laville-Haut-Brion
Meursault
Genevrières
Charmes
Goutte d'Or
Casse-Tête
Perrières
Pouligny-Montrachet
   Pucelles
   Cailleret
   Combettes
   Refert

Chassagne-Montrachet
   Ruchottes
   Caillerets
   Boudriottes
Aloxe-Corton
Clos des Mouches Blanc
Chablis:
   Vaudésir
   Les Clos
   Grenouilles
   Valmur
   Blanchots
   Les Preuses
   Bougros
Ch. de Saran
Ch. Chalon
Maximin Grünhauser Herrenberg
   Kabinett, Schubert
Scharzhofberger Kabinett, Egon Müller
Schloss Böckelheimer Kupfergrube
   Kabinett
Marqués de Murrieta Blanco
Neuchâtel, Château d'Auvernier
Fendant les Murettes
Aigle les Murailles
Tokay Aszu, 5 Puttonyos
Great Wall

Sparkling
Clairette de Die
Saumur
Vouvray
St.-Péray
Seyssel (Boyer Brut and Le Duc)
White Burgundy (Kriter)
Asti Spumanti, Cinzano
Champagnes:
   Mumm, Moët & Chandon, Piper
   Heidsieck, Heidsieck Monopole,
   Charles Heidsieck, Lanson, Ayala,
   Veuve-Cliquot, Krug, Pommery and
   Greno, Deutz and Geldermann, Dom
   Ruinart, Louis Roederer, Taittinger,
   Pol Roger, Perrier-Jouet, Bollinger,
   Laurent Perrier, Mercier

OVER $10

Red
Ch. Lafite-Rothschild
Ch. Latour
Ch. Mouton-Rothschild
Ch. Margaux
Ch. Haut-Brion
Ch. Ausone
Ch. Cheval Blanc
Ch. Petrus
Le Chambertin
Chambertin-Clos de Bèze
Bonnes Mares
Clos de Vougeot

Grande Rue
La Romanée
Échezeaux
Romanée-St. Vivant
Grands-Échezeaux
La Tâche
Richebourg
Romanée-Conti
Corton

White
Ch. Haut-Brion
Ch. d'Yquem
Corton-Charlemagne
Bienvenues-Bâtard-Montrachet
Bâtard-Montrachet
Chevalier-Montrachet
Montrachet
Crios-Bâtard-Montrachet
Condrieu
Château-Grillet

Sparkling
Vintage champagnes:
   Mumm, Moët & Chandon, Piper
   Heidsieck, Heidsieck Monopole,
   Charles Heidsieck, Lanson, Ayala,
   Veuve-Cliquot, Krug, Pommery and
   Greno, Deutz and Geldermann, Dom
   Ruinart, Louis Roederer, Taittinger,
   Pol Roger, Perrier-Jouet, Bollinger,
   Laurent Perrier, Mercier
Nazdorovya Extra Brut

Fortified

ABOUT $4

Florio Marsala—dry or sweet
Rivero Trocadero Amontillado
KWV Paarl Sherry

ABOUT $5
Justino Sercial

ABOUT $6
Domecq La Ina Fina
Gonzalez Byass Tio Pepe Fino
Williams & Humbert Dry Sack
Leacock Malmsey

ABOUT $7
Cossart Gordon Bual Madeira
Cockburn's Special Reserve Port
Sandeman's Partners' Port

ABOUT $8
Harvey's Bristol Cream

$10–$25
Vintage Ports:
   Hooper, Dow, Graham, Warre,
   Fonseca, Robertson, Sandeman,
   Quinta da Noval, Croft, A. J. da
   Silva, Taylor

INDEX

ACKNOWLEDGMENTS

In this space it would not be possible to acknowledge our indebtedness to all those who have furthered our effort. But special thanks must go to Barbara Ensrud, whose editorial support has proved invaluable in the creation of this book, and John Laird, researcher, organizer, and liaison between authors and publisher.

C. F.   S. A.

PICTURE CREDITS

Peter Aaron 11, 68, 88; Almadén Vineyards 18–20; Robert L. Balzer 24, 38, 42, 44, 50, 52, 72, 90, 107, 129, 133, 135; Bell & Stanton 10, 73, 103, 105, 106; Bettmann Archive 59; Dave Boss 40, 61, 62, 63; Browne Vintners 108; Bully Hill Vineyard 26; Rene Burri 70, 101; Jack Cakebread 39, 43, 44; Christian Brothers 4, 7 & 8, 14 & 15, 16, 27; Dreyfus, Ashby & Co. 138; Maison Joseph Drouhin 81; German Wine Information 114, 115, 126; Bárbara Haas 102; Percy Hennell 139, 141; Steve Kraft for Boordy Vineyards 60; Kunsthistorisches, Vienna, Photo Erwin Meyer 127; Arnold Newman 69, 71, 91; The Prado, Photo MAS 134; Seagram Company Ltd. 1974 Annual Report, Photo Phil Marco cover, 144; Sonoma Vineyards 45; James Thurber 13; Wine Institute 28.

Drawing by James Thurber From MEN, WOMEN AND DOGS, Published by Harcourt Brace Jovanovich. Copr. © 1943 James Thurber. Copr. © 1971 Helen W. Thurber and Rosemary Thurber Sauers. Originally printed in The New Yorker.
Maps by Robert Porter